P9-BZV-835

HOW TO HANDLE
PRESSURE

Clyde M.
How to handle
Ruth E.

Narramore

pressure

Narramore

TYNDALE HOUSE
Publishers, Inc.
Wheaton, Illinois

Coverdale House
Publishers, Ltd.
London, England

Library of Congress Catalog Card Number 75-7226. ISBN 8423-1513-6, cloth.
 First printing, July 1975. Printed in the United States of America

To
our dear children
MELODIE and KEVIN
whose consistent lives
and Christian conduct
have enabled us to live
with a minimum of
pressure

Contents

In all references to case histories,
the identities of original subjects
are completely disguised by changing
names, places, and other details.
No actual person living today is
described in any of these anecdotes.

Introduction

"Pressure! Who doesn't have it?"

This was the reaction of one man when he heard that we were writing this book.

He was right in that everyone experiences a certain amount of pressure. Of course, a *little* pressure can even be helpful. It can shake you out of your lethargy and spur you on to accomplishment. But real hard core pressure—the tension building, stress producing variety, is something to avoid.

Yet, can anyone escape pressure in the kind of world we live in today? Although this is the golden age of technological advances, there's a price to pay. Society hardly ever gives us an advantage without taking something in exchange. Improvements in housing, transportation, energy, communications, labor saving machinery and a host of remarkable devices have become our heritage. We applaud their coming with enthusiasm and great hope.

"Now life will be easier and better," we say.

But along with these "blessings" are burdens of financial debt and added responsibilities. Our mechanized way of life has supposedly brought us more leisure, but it's soon filled up with more work to make more money to buy more machines. Modern man keeps an unbelievable pace in a perpetual race—and wins a *trophy of pressure*.

People look longingly at TV shows where lucky winners are awarded fabulous travel prizes.

"Now you can get away from it all," the enthusiastic show host says. "You'll have a leisurely cruise to a beautiful island paradise in the South Seas."

INTRODUCTION

Sometimes we are deluded into believing that we can leave our pressures behind and find a utopia in some far away land where we'll have neither tension nor stress. A more relaxed way of life surely helps, but it's only half the answer to a complicated and involved problem.

It's hard to escape from pressure because we tend to carry it with us. Although a goodly share is caused by our environment, perhaps more is inside the mind and heart.

This book deals with both kinds of pressure: the outside and the inside. It explores pressure as it relates to a way of life.

The concepts in this book are not a panacea, but they are working in many families, and we trust they will be effective in your life as well.

Clyde M. Narramore
Ruth E. Narramore

I. What Are You Doing?

At a dinner honoring the seventieth birthday of the celebrated American writer, Mark Twain, he was called upon to make a speech. With a twinkle in his eye and the droll humor so typical of the man, he responded:

"I have achieved my seventy years in the usual way: by sticking strictly to a scheme of life which would kill anybody else. I have made it a rule to go to bed when there wasn't anybody left to sit up with; and I have made it a rule to get up when I had to. This has resulted in an unswerving regularity of irregularity."

Mark Twain was wrong in the assumption that he had a corner on this kind of routine. The reason his remarks tickle our funny bones is that many of us can identify with his "scheme of life." We know what he means when he refers to "an unswerving regularity of irregularity."

For Mark Twain, this haphazard life-style appeared to have worked. At least, we do know that he merited world-wide acclaim as a writer. His unstructured way of life seemed to match his "hang-loose" personality and homespun wit. He was a character with a touch of genius.

But most of us are not a Samuel Clemens. And since we are not endowed with any singular quality of genius, living a life that follows "an unswerving regularity of irregularity" can have some repercussions. Although it gives the overtones of a relaxed, unpressured existence, when the day of reckoning arrives, we find ourselves in a stew. Without planning, organizing, preparing and many other considerations dealt with throughout this book, the person with responsibilities will find himself snowed under by an avalanche of pressure.

2
HOW TO HANDLE PRESSURE

Evaluate Your Time

Strange as it may seem, everyone has the same amount of time: there are twenty-four hours around the clock. No matter where you are on this planet, you've got *equal time* with everyone else. But what you fill in those hours, and the way you go about it spells the difference between a well-ordered life and one that is characterized by tension and stress.

If you're one who manages to keep busy—*too* busy—but you don't know what happens to your time, it's a good idea to take inventory. Like packing a suitcase, you really can't organize it well unless you know what goes into it.

A child, in packing for a trip, may stuff his things into a suitcase, then sit on it to get it closed. But when his mother comes to check her offspring's progress, and catches a glimpse of the bulging bag with various articles of clothing hanging out through the cracks, she dumps the contents on the bed and begins to repack. As she puts things back in, she also does some organizing, neatly folding all foldable items and placing like things together. A few articles she may remove as being unnecessary (like empty gum wrappers and Coca-Cola bottle caps). Some essentials (like pj's and socks) may be lacking, so she adds them to the suitcase.

The amazing thing is what happens to that luggage after the mother has repacked it. Now that everything has been placed in the bag in an orderly, systematic way, there seems to be plenty of room. Shutting the suitcase now is no problem; it closes with ease.

If your day seems so packed that you can't fit everything into it without undue pressure, you probably need to sort out and rearrange your activities. The first step, as in packing a suitcase, is to take an inventory of what takes place during the course of the day. In this way you'll know exactly what and how much you are trying to put into it. Don't expect to do much about pressure until you sort out your activities by making a schedule, outlining every half hour throughout the day and evening, (7:00, 7:30, 8:00, 8:30, 9:00, 9:30, 10:00, etc. . . .). Keep right on through the morning, afternoon and evening, recording the many ways, big or little, in which you spend each half hour segment. If this is too difficult, try an hourly account. This may seem like a nuisance, but if you'll do this for a period of one week, you'll begin to develop a fairly clear picture of how you actually spend your time. Since you can't do much about rearranging your schedule until you've sorted out the contents, keeping this record will be worth the bother.

At the end of the week, you may be in for some surprises. But undoubtedly, you will have turned up some valuable discoveries about the way you spend your time. These, in turn, may offer important clues as to why tension and pressure infiltrate your life.

3
WHAT ARE YOU DOING?

Now, with the chart completed, you're ready to study it and make an objective evaluation of what you are doing with your time. Review your schedule with an open mind and ask yourself the following questions:

1. Which activities demand the most time? Do they take more of your time than they should?

2. Which ones require the least amount of time? Are any of them being neglected?

3. What determines your schedule? What factors influence your activities?

4. In what ways are you wasting time?

5. Are there many unanticipated demands on your time? If so, approximately how much time is used in this way?

6. What shortcuts can be used in doing your work?

7. Could some of your jobs be delegated to others?

8. Which activities do you find most enjoyable? Proportionately, how much time is spent on them?

9. Which activities do you find distasteful? How much time, comparatively, is given to doing unpleasant tasks?

10. In what areas do you feel the greatest amount of frustration and pressure?

11. Do you compensate in legitimate ways for the pressures you feel?

12. Whom do you blame when things go wrong?

13. How much time do you allow for relaxation and recreation?

14. Do you take time to eat regular, well-balanced meals?

15. Do you get a sufficient amount of sleep? What are your average hours of sleep per night? For the most part, is your sleep unbroken and satisfying?

16. How much time do you spend with your family on a non-work basis?

17. Do you seek God's guidance in your decisions, your problems and your concerns?

18. Do you have a quiet time with God each day? Do you systematically read His Word and pray?

When you've answered these questions (and others which may be especially meaningful to you), you will know if you need to "repack" your day. A little rearrangement of your time may alleviate a lot of pressure!

Is It Necessary?

You'd never dream of trying to squeeze your entire wardrobe and all your other belongings into one medium size suitcase. When you go on a trip, you must decide what you will need most and what is important to have with you.

4 HOW TO HANDLE PRESSURE

It's much the same with your time. There's so much to do and so much that you'd like to do. But time is not made of rubber; it won't stretch. Only so much can fit into your day. Of necessity, you must make choices.

Choosing the needed and the important is not always that simple. Our society has distorted human values by often placing a strong emphasis on things of relatively minor importance. The acquisition of fancy gadgets is substituted for family relationships. Social status and glamour rate higher than thoughtfulness and integrity. Financial resources are more sought after than godliness. When priorities become confused and off balance, people become targets for tension.

Wrong choices are always flanked by pressure. But when struggling in the midst of stress and strain, people are prone to accuse circumstances or someone else for their pressured predicaments. It's often difficult to recognize one's own blame in making the wrong choices.

Martha was a classic example. Very graciously she had opened her home to a houseful of guests. One of them was Jesus: the others were His disciples. Naturally, she was excited about having them there and she was anxious for everything to be just right. My, she was busy! You have to admit that preparing a dinner for thirteen or more extra men when you're accustomed to cooking for only three (and two of them, women), is definitely work.

The problem was that she had no help. At least, this is what Martha thought. There she was, dashing between the kitchen and dining room, setting the table, keeping the biscuits from burning, and trying to do a dozen things at once. If only she had more help! There was too much to do alone.

It might not have bothered Martha so much if she hadn't been resentful inside because of her sister's apparent thoughtlessness. She *needed* Mary's help. There was no question about that. But Mary, it seemed, had dismissed all responsibility and was sitting with the guests enjoying herself.

You can hardly blame Martha for being upset. But when she asked Jesus to reprimand Mary for her negligence, she was in for a big surprise.

"Martha, Martha," He lovingly answered, "you are worried and bothered about so many things; but only a few things are necessary, really *only* one" (Luke 10:41, 42). Then Jesus went on to explain that Mary had made the right choice. The one *necessary* thing was not food, but fellowship with Christ. This is what Mary had chosen.

How easy it is to become "worried and bothered about so many things!" They may be *good* things, but not "necessary." The "necessary" is your first priority. It supersedes all else, no matter how desirable other things appear.

So when you're pressured and overwhelmed by more work than you have time, ask yourself if it's necessary. When you weed out the unnecessary, your priorities will fall into place, and your pressures will diminish!

2. Fit As a Fiddle

Karen had everything going for her. As a pretty coed at the State University, she was popular, vivacious and ambitious. She kept up her grades as an honor student even though actively participating in sports and a host of other student activities.

But during the past few months, something had gone awry. Karen was not herself. She continually complained of being tired and was often irritable and despondent. Everything became a burden and each assignment developed into a major crisis.

One by one, she dropped her extra-curricular activities. She dropped out of sports, and even dropped one of her major classes. But, when the mid-semester grades came out, that's when the big blow hit. This was the first time in Karen's college career that she had failed to make the dean's list. She felt utterly disgraced and hopeless.

That night she phoned home and sobbed out her tale of woe to her concerned parents. They encouraged her to take a still lighter schedule the next semester and urged her to see a doctor. Karen's examination by the school physician revealed no apparent reason for her poor health. Then, one evening a few weeks later, she phoned her parents again and shocked them by blurting out: "I'm quitting school. It's just too much pressure. I can't get my assignments in on time and I'm getting so far behind that it's positively hopeless. Maybe I should see a psychiatrist or something. I wish I were dead!" Then she lost her composure and the tears spilled out freely over the emotional dam that had been holding them in check.

By the next day, Karen's parents had arrived at her dorm to take her home. Feeling strongly that their daughter's problem was physical rather than emotional, they arranged for her to visit a clinic for extensive testing. When the test for glucose tolerance was administered, it showed that Karen was the victim of low blood sugar, a condition known as hypoglycemia. Her doctor immediately put her on a strict high-protein diet. Within a short time there was a decided change for the better. With continued improvement, Karen was soon able to return to college and finish the school year with flying colors.

It was evident from Karen's experience that pressures which she ordinarily took in stride, became unbearable shackles when she was physically down. This is true of everyone. Women have a reputation for liking to shop, but shopping can become a burden when a woman doesn't feel well. It's folly not to recognize the relevancy of pressure and physical health.

Even a headache or fatigue can distort your perspectives. Although you may normally have a gregarious personality and enjoy the company of others, when your head is pounding or you're exhausted from lack of sleep, unexpected visitors can be pretty hard to take. Tomorrow, when you're rested and feel better, it will be a different story.

Pressure Capacity

The weight of pressure is not only judged by the size of the load but by the strength of the one who bears it.

A heavy crate can be carried by a large truck with ease, but that same crate when placed upon a child's wagon will crush it. The weaker wagon cannot sustain the heavy weight of pressure that is placed upon it. So it is with your physical well-being. When you suffer from poor health, you are overwhelmed by pressures that are not even considered as such by others who enjoy vibrant health.

Think of it this way. Your health is something like a bridge. If it is sturdy and strong, it can sustain a heavy load; if it is weak, even a lesser load may cause it to collapse.

It's simple logic to recognize that the stronger you are, the more pressure you can bear; and the weaker or more fragile you are, the less you can tolerate. Your physical well-being has a direct bearing upon your reaction to the pressures of life. Poor health places life in a framework of pressure, while good health accepts it as a challenge. How you feel physically affects your sense of pressure more than you probably realize.

Remember times when you felt like a million dollars—wonderful, tremendous! You were convinced you could jump over the moon if you needed to. You felt you could tackle almost anything and it wouldn't throw you.

7
FIT AS A FIDDLE

Then there were those other days: you didn't feel so well, you were tired and your head ached. These were the times, of course, when everything went wrong. At least it seemed that way. Molehills became mountains and any little thing could get you down.

People need stimulation in order to find motivation. Yet, when you're in a fragile physical state, any task demanding initiative becomes a stressful situation. Responsibility takes on the dimension of pressure. It doesn't take much to throw on the panic switch or cause you to crumble.

Your human body, however, is an amazingly flexible organism. It learns to adapt to its shortcomings. Through the years, it may have had its problems, not functioning as efficiently as it should. Perhaps you needed medication or a different diet, or some other corrective measures. Nevertheless, since change is gradual (and therefore subtle), it is easy to accustom yourself to feeling badly. In other words, you develop a tolerance which accepts your physical problems as natural for you. It's entirely possible to feel below par most of the time, and yet not be aware of your low-level physical condition. If you would turn the calendar back to relive a day or a week of your life 20, 10, or even 5 years ago, you might be amazed at the difference between how you felt then and the way you drag around now.

So if pressures are getting you down, take a close look at your health. Do you have enough physical stamina to hold up under the stress and strains of life? Do routine responsibilities that others accept without batting an eyelash leave you feeling on the bottom of the pile? If everything you do turns out to be a big energy crisis—*your* energy—chances are that your supply needs medical assistance. You weren't meant to drag around feeling like a flat tire under a two-ton truck. If that's the way you find it, it's time you take some action.

Not Perfect, but the Best You Have

Your body, fantastic mechanism that it is, must be kept in good running order if it is to operate with maximum efficiency. "The maimed, the halt and the blind," are not the only ones struggling against physical handicaps. True, theirs are the most obvious, and undoubtedly, the most serious: yet, in a sense we all are forced to live with physical malfunctions. Ever since the fall of our first ancestors in the Garden of Eden, the human body has fought to surmount the effects of the curse.

No human organism is immune to disorders. But since the body of the believer is the "temple" of the Holy Spirit, the Christian, above all persons, has the serious responsibility of keeping the "temple" in good repair. It is difficult to live well in an inadequate house. So, also, if we are to effectively fulfill our obligations to God, ourselves, and those about us, we must recognize the influence of the house (human body) upon the life-style of its occupant, (the ego). An inefficient home is a pressure prone place, while a well-ordered domain creates an atmosphere of peace and well-being. Similarly, an unhealthy body *predisposes* an individual towards pressure and undue stress, while a healthy body tends to *protect* one from harmful pressures. Therefore, to avoid an emotional climate of stress, it is essential to keep your body in as good a condition as your physical limitations allow.

Your Habits Are Showing

Good health is often the result of good habits. When you follow the three R's of health and "Live Right—Eat Right—and Sleep Right," you've got a running start. To "Live Right" you must be at peace with God, yourself, and the world around you. This means that God is directing your life, and you are following his blueprint for living. It's fool-proof, tried and tested by multitudes who have experienced His amazing grace. It's been proven that the Christian has fewer health problems than the unregenerate. This is the reason why certain insurance companies charge Christians a lower premium rate: they are lower risks.

Gourmet

It is often said that "you are what you eat." This is not entirely accurate, since you don't become a hot-dog just because you've devoured a weiner. But the nutrients you put into your body—the vitamins and minerals supplied through a balanced diet—are essential to your physical well-being. Without the proper amount of these, your body is in trouble.

It's a known fact that in our advanced twentieth century, in the midst of plenty, there are thousands who suffer from malnutrition. These victims, however, are not necessarily the poor and needy. In fact, a large segment of the undernourished are found in our affluent upper societies.

It's not that these people can't afford the proper foods. They don't want them. Growing children and teen-agers, it seems, much prefer candy (especially chocolate), ice cream or rich pastries to fruit. Pizza and spaghetti are far more popular than old-fashioned meat and vegetables, and sugar-filled coke has held the national title for the number one soft drink beverage for a whole generation of young people. Balanced meals, for many youngsters, have been replaced by junk. Why not, they reason, when that's what they like and they have the money to spend for it!

Unfortunately, their permissive parents don't do much better. The pattern, it appears, is one that alternates between rich calorie-laden gourmet specialties and starvation rations designed to quickly take off the excess poundage acquired by the rich food routine. Fad diets in America have become the pastime of the sophisticated. Yet many of the suggested so-called miracle diets are extremely lopsided in nutritive benefits and are, as such, a menace to one's health.

It was neither an accident nor an act of fate which caused Karen, the pretty coed discussed earlier, to become afflicted with hypoglycemia. Karen, as you recall, had been caught up in a whirlwind of college activities. In fact, she became too busy to eat—or so she thought! So she began meal-skipping. Then to silence her growling stomach, she filled up with candy, potato chips, cokes and all kinds of other popular non-nutrients. After a time of such nutritional neglect, it was little wonder that her system experienced serious repercussions.

Forty Winks

Sleeping Right, the third "R" of good health, is one that is often short-changed. Yet, the value of sleep goes far beyond your feeling of alertness. Sleep is essential to your physical and emotional restoration since it is during your sleeping hours that the process of rejuvenation takes place. In the Magic Kingdoms of Disneyland and Disneyworld, part of the charm pervading these delightful parks lies in a continuing, fresh, new, well-cared-for impression. Everything is kept in ship-shape condition and wear and tear just doesn't seem to exist. What is more, during all the times I have visited the Magic Kingdoms over the years, I have never seen a repair crew. I mentioned this observation to a friend who was employed at Disneyland.

"Disneyland is in continual repair," he answered, "but it's not intended that you nor any other visitor should see the process. At the close of each day, after the guests have left, the maintenance crews arrive. Throughout the night and into the early morning hours, they work like eager beavers, painting, gardening, repairing and rejuvenating the various attractions, buildings and landscape. By 9:30 A.M. when the park officially opens to the public, the workmen are gone. But they will return again that evening."

Your body follows much the same pattern. The sleep hours (when you are not responsible to the "public"), follow the taxing routine of the day, restoring and refreshing your mind and body in preparation for another busy routine the next day. No wonder God declares that "we are fearfully and wonderfully made" (Psalm 139:14).

Another imperative in your quest for good health is a consistent pattern of physical exercise. In today's urban living, exercise is seldom part of a daily routine unless you deliberately make provision for it. The body was never intended to be sedentary: it was made for movement. To ignore this is asking for trouble. Of course, exercise is something you work up to—not jump into. Too much too soon can cause serious harm. But moderate exercise *is* essential for the normal, healthy body that you need to shield you from the squeeze of stress.

There is no substitute for taking good care of yourself. Since you alone know how you feel, it is your responsibility to keep yourself in good physical condition. A person who is particular about the condition of his car takes it to a mechanic for periodic check-ups to be sure it's in good running order. If it needs repair, he has the work done right away. A car isn't worth much compared to a person; yet many neglect their health and do not get proper medical attention. It's not pampering yourself to have regular physical check-ups. It's the only body you'll have here on earth. Take care of it.

I remember a man used to say, "No one ought to feel worse than he should!" This may be "butternut wisdom" but it's also a worthy truism. In other words, you owe it to yourself to feel as well as you can, considering your individual physical makeup. So if your "pressure" gauge indicates that you're not feeling your best, it's time that you take your health seriously.

3. Conflicts Within

One day I was flying on a jet between California and Florida. The stewardess, noticing that I was writing, asked, "Writing a book?"

"Well, actually I am."

"What is it about?" she asked.

"It has to do with emotional problems," I said.

"Almost everyone has some emotional hangups, don't you think?" she asked.

Being a psychologist, I didn't answer her question. Instead, I asked, "What do you mean?"

"Well," she explained, "Nearly everyone I know has some kind of emotional problem."

Then she began to tell me about some of her friends. "I've got this one girl friend," she said, "who is, a, well, she's a terrific gal, but every so often she gets down in the dumps and really gets depressed. She's OK most of the time, but when she has these bad days, I really feel sorry for her."

The stewardess continued to tell about several of her other friends who were obviously insecure, withdrawn, or hostile, or who suffered from some other emotional disturbance. As she continued to talk I sensed that she undoubtedly had some problems herself! Of course she was right in that everyone has at least a few emotional problems. This is part of being a human being. But some people, in fact, millions, have moderate or even serious disturbances.

Emotional conflicts bring tenseness. They interfere with your progress and happiness. To be laden with unresolved problems is like trying to put a jigsaw puzzle together when several parts are missing. Nothing seems to come out right. No matter how hard you try, things just don't seem to fit. And the result is pressure.

When Love Is Not There

One day I was speaking to a group of women about emotional problems. During the discussion period a well-dressed lady asked a question about her son, Bobby.

After considering the problem, she asked very pointedly, "What should I do? How can I handle this? Do you have any suggestions?"

We discussed the problem further, then I suggested she might consider telling her son, each day, that she loved him.

"You might say, 'Bobby, I love you so much.' "

At that point the lady flinched, her upper body shaking momentarily. I could see immediately that such a suggestion would never suit her.

"You wouldn't find it easy, would you, to openly tell Bobby you loved him?"

"Oh, no," she said, "he knows I love him, and—well, I just couldn't say things outright like that."

"It would be difficult for you to tell him pointedly that you love him?"

"That's right," she said, "I couldn't do that."

Then I asked her about her own relationship with her father when she was growing up. I asked her if he regularly held her on his lap and hugged her and kissed her and told her point blank how much he loved her.

"Oh, no," she said, in a rather nervous, uncomfortable voice, "he never did anything like that. He wasn't that kind of a man. I can't remember him ever telling me he loved me."

Then we discussed the fact that open expression of love was foreign to her experience; it seemed so unnatural and awkward. I'm sure some of the women in that audience were shocked to think that a mother couldn't tell her child she loved him. Undoubtedly many of them had been raised in homes where their parents had expressed love freely. They had grown up feeling they were loved, and now they could easily tell their children they loved them.

But with this woman it was different. And so it is with untold numbers of mothers, fathers, teachers and other adults. They cannot spontaneously tell another person they love them. And this brings tremendous anxiety and stress into a person's life. A parent should be able to love his child and tell him so. But if he cannot, it brings strained relations between the parent and the child. And, of course, it goes much farther than that. If a mother can't tell a child she loves him, she probably cannot tell her *husband* she loves *him*. So they may go through life bound up like mummies. This brings enormous pressure to a marriage. Such a mother, for example, may see that her husband "doesn't do the right thing," or that "Bobby is not turning out well." Nearly everything becomes a burden. Yet the mother may not realize that her own emotional problems bring on this lifetime of pressure.

Things We Imagine

Not long ago a man wrote me about his deep feelings of depression. They had become so severe that he really didn't want to live. A portion of his letter read like this:

"I very much need help for my mind and imagination. My thinking has just about destroyed me. The things I imagine are real to me and seem like the truth; but people think I'm crazy.

"If there is any way you can help me, please send me information. I was in despair this past week and ready to take my own life, but the Lord really used your radio broadcasts during this difficult time. You discussed a problem like mine. You will never know what understanding and insight can do to help a person keep on keeping on."

From this letter you can well understand that this man has deep disturbances. In fact, he has said that he had seriously considered taking his own life. To a person who has never had emotional problems, such a condition may seem extremely bizarre. In fact, most people with normal feelings would never understand why another person would want to end his own life. But to the person who is deeply disturbed, "ending it all" seems the only thing to do to alleviate his intense suffering from which he seems unable to escape.

Needless to say, feelings such as this man described bring continued pressure on him. He can't really get anything done because he's preoccupied with his own disturbance. Fortunately such people can receive professional help and get well. Many people have done just that.

Teen-Agers Too

I suppose most people think that adults are the only ones who suffer from severe emotional problems. But this is far from true. Emotional disturbances are not limited to grown-ups. They plague children and young people as well. This letter from a teen-age girl shows how confused a young person can be.

14 HOW TO HANDLE PRESSURE

"I am a seventeen-year-old girl, living at home, and my father is dead. I am confused and mixed up. I was saved a few months ago, but it seemingly has no meaning for me. I have kept on doing the things I did before. There isn't any desire to do right. I'm really miserable.

"I'm beginning to hate myself. I heard once that if you can't be a Christian at home, you can't be one anywhere.

"My mother has gone to church but has dropped out. I don't know if she's a Christian or not. If she is, I wish she'd offer some help once in a while. We have never been close, and I'm the only girl at home (but there are three brothers). There's a barrier between us and I can't knock it down by myself.

"We take care of three welfare children. People tell us that we're doing a great thing, but I can't help feeling jealous. Mom has three welfare kids to give her love to, and by the time she gets to me there's no love left.

"Whenever I feel I'm not loved I get very depressed. My pastor told me I had to bring myself out of it. But I can't do it by myself.

"I will graduate from high school in June, and I can hardly wait. Christmas is supposed to be a time of happiness and sharing, but each year it has only brought me misery and loneliness. Please help!"

We often think of childhood days as "carefree" days. But with many young people this time of life produces a continual nightmare. Evidently the basic need for feeling loved has never been met in this girl's life. Her father is not living, and she has no desirable relationship with her mother. The welfare children are evidently occupying the mother's attention so that this girl feels all the more rejected and alone, and she says, "there's no love left." She's depressed, confused, and lonely. These terrible feelings gnaw away at her, bringing constant pressure. And the outlook for such a girl is not good unless someone senses her special needs and begins to relate to her positively over a period of time.

We often see young people like this seventeen-year-old girl, around church, going back and forth to school, but we may not realize the terrible agony inside their hearts. Almost any well-adjusted person could help this girl by being friendly to her and encouraging her to talk. But if she does not relate to someone in the near future, her emotional disturbances are likely to take a greater toll on her. In fact, before too long, she may be spending every spare penny for psychiatric services or for hospitalization.

What's Wrong With Me?

A person may have severe conflicts and yet never really pinpoint what the precise problem is. He may feel it is the person he has to live with, or he may think the government is to blame, or he may feel that God doesn't like him. It's a great day in a person's life when he gets enough insight to understand his basic emotional disturbance. Until then, he cannot begin working on it.

Not long ago I received this letter which shows how a little insight has helped a woman to understand her conflicts within.

"I have just finished reading your booklet entitled *The Many Faces of Bitterness*. If it didn't sound so *spooky* I'd say for sure that God put this booklet in my hands!*

"For years I have been searching, reading, studying—trying so hard to find out what it is in me that makes me act and react the way I do.

"Serious illness, tragic deaths of loved ones, and financial reverses (through no fault of my own) have been my lot. I am a sixty-nine-year-old widow (no living children) living in a small mobile-home park. To make ends meet I pick up clean, secondhand magazines and newspapers where people who have finished with them discard them. Then I sell them.

"Yesterday, I picked up a magazine. Tucked inside was your booklet. I started to discard it but decided to read it instead. As I read it and re-read it, I saw that my problem was actually bitterness. Now I see more clearly how bitter I really am. I guess it shows up in nearly everything I do. I liked the part on the causes. I saw myself on every page. This helps so much. Just knowing and understanding helps a lot. I guess you'd say that I can live with myself a little better. Any further information will help me. I believe that if I had a few counseling sessions like you suggested at one place in the booklet, I might get over this problem entirely. I will start working on it at once, but I'll need some help. Where can I hear you on the radio, and when? Any information would be so greatly appreciated."

My heart goes out for this dear lady whose life of misery has been a mystery to her. She says she has been reading, studying, and trying to find out what has been making her feel the way she did. But naturally she couldn't detach herself from her life and stand aside on a little hill and look objectively at herself. She only knew that she was caught in an unhappy web and she was fighting to get out. This is so characteristic.

Through the years I have received many thousands of letters from people who have heard our daily broadcast, "Psychology for Living." As I discussed problems they were evidently led to insights which helped them to understand why they were feeling as they were. It was as though a large window suddenly appeared and shed important light on their understanding. Such was the case of the foregoing lady who came to understand that her

*The booklet *The Many Faces of Bitterness* is available without charge by writing: Narramore Christian Foundation, Rosemead, California 91770.

confusion and pain were related to her deep feelings of bitterness. Now she can start looking in the right direction for the help she needs. But it is tragic that she has had to wait until she was nearly seventy years of age to gain this insight. Her years of life have been filled with undue pressure and anxiety because of this emotional disturbance.

In Search of Identity

In the early months and years of life a child may be subjected to extreme emotional deprivation because he was not wanted. In many instances such a child may have been adopted by a good family and yet suffer from the loss of early and continued love. In many cases, adopted children are raised by loving parents. On the other hand, an adopted child may be raised by well-meaning parents who seem unable to meet the child's needs. In fact, they may have some problems of their own which are reflected in the youngster's disturbance. Of course, such conditions could persist in *any* home. The following letter received from a woman reveals the unusual concern she has for her adopted daughter, who has been married and divorced three times. Now, at 29, the daughter is still wondering who she is and why she was rejected in her early months of life.

"Some months ago you spoke in our city and I was present in your audience. I asked about parents having special problems with adopted children and you gave a most understanding answer.

"In our case we adopted a daughter when she was nearly a year old. During her early years she was a joy to us but as she grew older I often felt she was trying to destroy herself. She quit college in her second year to marry a very immature boy who had been raised by his grandparents who also were mixed up emotionally. At his mother's divorce, the father took one child and the mother took the other, but the father turned the boy over to the grandparents and the child could never understand why.

"My daughter was already divorced when she finally told us they were separated. She then married another boy, actually mentally lacking, and divorced him four months before a child was born. We helped our daughter financially and I also helped care for the child when she went back to work.

"Again, she married a much older man who already was three times divorced, but telling us months after. They've now moved to another state.

"We do not ask, what did we do wrong—we really tried hard to be good Christian parents. We still stand beside her and love her although there is no actual communication between us. Now that she is twenty-nine, she still asks the question, 'Who am I, and why was I given out for adoption?'

"Please send me booklet No. 3 about adoption which you have mentioned on the radio.*

"I wish I knew how I could help her."

We do not know, of course, what took place in this family. Evidently the parents did the best they knew. What they did might have been mostly right and it may have even been mostly wrong. The child may have had physical disabilities which predisposed her toward emotional problems. These facts we do not know, but we are sure of one thing: the child grew up to become a disturbed person whose life has been marked by failure and constant pressure. The daughter needs help. But the parents need help, too. They are suffering and wondering what went wrong. They must harbor deep feelings of guilt and bewilderment. Their dearest project has failed and they can't understand the reason for the shambles.

Not long ago I was talking with a woman about the importance of a good parental relationship in childhood. Immediately she said, "I can relate to this. When I was a child my father didn't tell me he loved me. He didn't like girls. In fact, he wouldn't look at me when I was born because he wanted a boy. He came to the hospital to bring my mother. He paid the bill, and as soon as he learned that I was a girl, he left the hospital and said he didn't want to look at me. So he went on home.

"But he didn't have any boys, just three girls. Consequently, in order to relate I had to learn to do things which boys did. This was the only way I could get any attention. Since he liked sports, I made it my business to be interested in all sports. In a sense I did my best to be a boy, but I failed, and never earned his attention. It was not until we were grown that Dad matured and mellowed, and indicated that he loved us. But it was too late. I already bore the scars of emotional deprivation of childhood."

With such an emotionally deprived childhood, it is a wonder this lady grew up to be as normal and fine as she is. But you can imagine the pressure this girl was under as she was growing up, to say nothing of the pressures she has sensed as an adult.

Solid Solutions

Emotional disturbances come in many sizes, from mild to severe. Last night, for example, I received a phone call from a lady in New Jersey. Evidently she was restless and unable to sleep, so she called me at 5:15 A.M. But she didn't realize that at my home in California, the clock read 2:15

*Booklet No. 3, *The Psychology of Adoption*, is available without charge by writing the Narramore Christian Foundation, Rosemead, California 91770.

A.M. I finally got my eyes and ears open enough to listen to her attentively. It soon became apparent that this woman was *not* just mildly disturbed. She had severe problems. She had been in and out of mental institutions for years. Her thinking was grossly impaired. Undoubtedly there was a time when her disturbances were minor. But because she did not receive help, and because the circumstances which produced her mental illness were not alleviated, she became progressively worse. This, however, is not always the case. A person may have little personality hang-ups which will remain about the same throughout life. Consequently, treatment for emotional disturbances varies from person to person, depending upon such factors as the nature of the disturbance, its severity, and the person's resources.

The first step in the treatment of emotional disturbances should usually be to see a medical doctor. Since all human beings are physiological beings, and since no one's body functions perfectly, there are many possibilities of physiological factors affecting how a person feels.

We know, for example, that some emotional problems can be traced to neurological impairments.* We know, also, that many emotional problems can be related to a variety of glandular dysfunctions. And so the list goes on and on—medical factors affecting one's emotional and mental well-being. It is often wise to seek help not only from a general practitioner but also from a medical *specialist*. Many people have sought psychological help for their problems, when actually the basic cause was physical in nature. After years of ineffective treatment, they have found that their problem was really physiologically-oriented.

But there are more than medical causes and medical solutions to problems. There are *spiritual* causes and solutions. People are not only physical beings, they are also spiritual beings. We are all made in the likeness and image of God, and have a capacity for God (Genesis 7:26-28). There are many spiritual factors which affect our feelings toward ourselves. As we feel differently (better) towards ourselves, we begin to perceive others differently, and we are relieved of many pressures.

Spiritual adequacy starts at the cross of Calvary. As we sense our need of a Savior, we can accept Christ, God's Son, as our personal redeemer and Lord. At that moment God forgives our sins, takes us into His family and His Holy Spirit dwells within our hearts. This new spiritual birth has a profound effect upon the total person.

*For a discussion of neurological factors relating to personality adjustment, see the author's book *Encyclopedia of Psychological Problems*, published by Zondervan, Grand Rapids, Michigan.
A booklet, *Children with Nervous and Emotional Problems*, is available without charge from the Narramore Christian Foundation, Rosemead, California 91770.

19 CONFLICTS WITHIN

Trusting Christ as personal Savior—being born again—does not solve all problems, because a person is more than a spirit fluttering around the room. He also has a body with many possible physiological problems and solutions. He is also an emotional being with psychological needs and solutions.

When a child comes into the world his whole being cries out for the fulfillment of basic emotional needs, such as love, security, and feeling that he is worthy.* If these needs are met quite well by those who raise him—usually his mother and father—he will develop healthy feelings toward himself and consequently toward others.

But if a person is raised by parents who, knowingly or unknowingly, do not meet these needs, he will absorb these negative attitudes, which tend to become a part of his personality. These attitudes carry over into adulthood, causing many problems. They cause him to have emotional hang-ups, or personality problems such as we have discussed in this chapter.

Healthy emotional development starts the day a child is born. During his "crystallizing" (youthful) years these attitudes become quite fixed for life. They are then difficult to change. But they *can* be changed. For example, a person can surrender his life to Christ, then begin to take his cues accurately from the Bible rather than from people in his childhood.

But some people need more than this; they need professional help in understanding their feelings, and in getting untangled. God often uses people to help people. It must please God to see people using the services of other people. God gives talent to people to do certain jobs. He gives counselors abilities so they can counsel, and God rarely does for people what they can do for themselves.

In summary, emotional conflicts bring on pressures in daily living. In fact, tensions may even engulf people but they may not realize that the real culprit is *conflict within*. As we become aware of our disturbances, we can then begin to do something about them. We can seek medical attention, spiritual assistance, or psychological help. And in time life will be enriched and happy, and many of the pressures will be resolved.

*The author's book *This Way to Happiness* deals with the basic emotional needs of man. It is available at all Christian bookstores, and from the Narramore Christian Foundation, Rosemead, California 91770.

4. Ready and Able

In Victor Herbert's charming operetta *Babes in Toyland*, Barnaby's young niece, Jane, struggles laboriously to find the answer to an arithmetic problem, only to meet with consistent failure. After numerous tries—all unsuccessful—she throws in the towel and defiantly sings out, "I don't care what the teacher says; I can't do that sum."

The Impossible Sum

There are thousands of youngsters in our school system who, like Jane, are chanting, "I can't do that sum." But a success-oriented society has no place for quitters. And teachers and parents, along with a host of others, respond to this frustration with the admonition, "If at first you don't succeed, try, try again." "Remember, if you 'try harder' you can become number one." Little wonder, then, that *grades* have become the goal of the status-seeking student. This push for perseverance and a better scholastic performance is probably needed by most children. Yet, for the "slow learner" or "below average" youngster the push to "do that sum" becomes a point of penetrating pressure.

Continued pressure, of course, looks for an escape valve which can show up in a variety of forms. The child might be emotionally upset, continually on the verge of tears. He may withdraw into the shelter of his own private world, or he may become hostile and strike out. On the other hand, he may resort to cheating in order to "achieve" what is expected of him. He may also try to gain recognition by clowning or through some other form of unacceptable behavior. Another youngster develops a nervous tic, gets sick to his stomach or has an attack of asthma. The damaging evidence of pressure comes through with scores of tell-tale symptoms.

We often fail to recognize the tremendous pressure that weighs upon our children. If we think of childhood simply as a carefree time with no worries, then our memories are too short. Children have very real concerns and are often not in a position to cope with them.

Chief among juvenile pressures is that which is brought on by the demands and expectations of ambitious adults. Actually, children *want* to comply. One of their earliest life-discoveries is that it is wise and prudent to stay in the good graces of authority. They find that it doesn't pay to incur adult displeasure. And so they try to meet the demands we place upon them. This is all well and good providing that we remain sensitive to the innate abilities and individual maturation levels of our youngsters. As long as we do not demand the impossible, it is good to encourage progress and development.

Danger lurks, however, in not discerning the limitations which could handicap the performance level of our children. Quite naturally, as parents we look for *our* children to shine bigger and better—(or at least, no less)—than other children their age. When they don't make it, we are keenly disappointed and quick to register our disapproval. Unwittingly, perhaps, we tend to pit them against their peers with such pressure quips as, "If Johnny can do it, why can't you?" We make unrealistic demands, combined with unreasonable threats if our children do not come across with an all-star performance. We require A's when a child may not be capable of more than a B, or even a C at that point in his intellectual development. We insist that Susie slave over a violin when, in fact, she has little or no talent for music. P.E. coaches are often among the most insensitive in reacting to lacks in a child's physical development and natural endowments. Boys, especially, who can't make the grade in athletics are often downgraded and humiliated to the point of causing them to feel extremely inferior. All of this adds up to pressure—lots of it.

I do not belittle the human need for motivation, but solid research tells us that incentive is a much healthier channel than fear. Fear is a deadly form of pressure, whereas incentive is an active form of hope—an outgrowth of encouragement. Fear is restrictive and crippling, while incentive is freeing. When we set unreachable goals for our children and cling to unrealistic expectations, the pressures that our children sense are those of fear. Little wonder, then that in their frustrations they sometimes rebel by shouting, like Jane, "I can't do that sum!"

23 READY AND ABLE

Misplaced Persons

But children aren't the only ones who wrestle with this kind of frustration. Adults, too, are often stymied by an impossible "sum." In other words, you find yourself trying to accomplish tasks which are out of your realm. When the job you are attempting exceeds the comfortable level of your ability, it causes you to feel insecure and becomes a source of pressure. It may be a big thing, or it might be something small. Perhaps you're concerned about that speech you've been asked to give at the next PTA meeting. Public speaking is not your bag, and you know it. Just thinking about speaking in front of those people makes you feel uptight and tense. It might not pressure someone else, but it does you. For another person, a pressure-concern might involve singing a solo, or entertaining the boss for dinner. Or you may be worried about those sticky monthly sales quotas. Perhaps you're wondering how you ever got to be a salesman in the first place. You don't seem to have what it takes. All of it, of course, adds up to undue pressure and stress.

When Tom, a young executive, recently received a promotion to a more responsible position in his firm, his friends congratulated him. Actually, if etiquette had permitted, condolences would have been more appropriate. Although Tom now had several men working under him, he was *not* executive material. He was good at following orders, but he had never liked to give them. He was mild-mannered and soft-spoken and the men in his department had a difficult time accepting his uncertain leadership. All in all, Tom was uncomfortable in his new position. Everything was a strain because his abilities did not match his responsibilities. As a result, pressure and stress characterized his working hours. Tom's advancement taxed his ability to the point of excessive stress. He was now a prime candidate for ulcers and other physical as well as emotional problems.

Elaine, the busy mother of three young children, was the organist at a small neighborhood church. Although she was not a great musician, she enjoyed playing and serving in this way. But when a new music director arrived and announced that the choir would be doing Handel's *Messiah* for the Christmas musical, Elaine went to pieces. She knew that this music was far beyond her ability and that, with family responsibilities, she would have little time to learn and practice something that difficult. The director was firm in his choice, however, so Elaine decided there was no alternative but for her to resign. But organists in that rural community were hard to come by, so the music committee prevailed upon her to remain and "just do the best she could."

As the rehearsals got under way, Elaine struggled and stumbled through the pages of the oratorio. Although the choir was not as aware of her mistakes as she was, she suffered untold embarrassment and wrestled with the anxiety and concern that she would be the cause of a gigantic musical fiasco. The pressure was tremendous. When the day of the performance arrived, Elaine was so upset that she became sick to her stomach. Fortunately for the choir, they were able to import a guest organist from a neighboring city. He was an accomplished musician, thoroughly familiar with the organ score of the *Messiah*. To him the performance presented no undue pressure because he possessed the training and ability to accomplish his task with ease. For Elaine, however, her tensions snowballed into trauma.

When a person finds himself in a position where everything is a strain, it is obvious that the job he's attempting is too much for him. There may be one of two reasons for this: (1) he needs more training and/or experience, (2) he does not have the mental and/or physical capacity or the natural aptitude required for the job. Struggling to perform a task which is beyond one's capability is the ultimate in frustration. Yet, there are many thousands of "misplaced persons" who belabor the handicap of being in the wrong kind of work.

Aptitudes

For many years, American automobile manufacturers have been marketing "job rated" trucks. Their lines include many sizes and kinds of trucks—each intended for a specific purpose. Some can carry lighter or heavier loads, or go places and do things the others cannot.

In a sense, people resemble these "job rated" trucks. They have different talents and abilities to fill a variety of needs. This is not to say that one person is more important or less worthy than anyone else. It *does* mean, however, that not everyone is cut out to do every kind of work.

When a person is blessed with unusual talent, there isn't much question about where his aptitudes lie; they stand right out. But that's not a description of the rank and file in today's world. What about Jack or Jill Average? How can such persons discover the extent of their strengths and limitations? Is there any way to find out what one's abilities really are? Many young people want to train for what will be their life's work, but they are in a quandary as to which direction they should go.

From the time a small child is able to talk, adults keep asking, "What do you want to be when you grow up?" Their childish ambitions run the gamut

25
READY AND ABLE

from "fireman," "nurse," "dog-catcher," to "taco salesman." Most youngsters change their minds over and over again. By the time they are ready for college, however, society expects them to have crystallized their goals. Unfortunately, the majority still aren't certain as to what they plan "to be." The pressure of choosing a college major bears down and forces these young people to make a choice. But they still aren't sure, and consequently, about half of the collegians who continue their studies change their majors, many of them several times. Even after all of this, a large number of these college grads will end up in jobs that do not suit them. The results, of course, will be pressure, causing a variety of emotional maladjustments.

What is the answer? How can you find your niche? Today there are numerous aptitude tests which often reveal hidden talents and inclinations. They are fairly accurate indicators of your weak areas as well as your strengths. To pursue a field that is centered around your natural aptitudes is to minimize the chance of being trapped in the pressure pot of the wrong kind of work.

It is customary among schools that offer training for various professions to require entrance examinations which screen students who do not have sufficient background or aptitude for that particular type of work. In most medical schools, for example, applicants are seldom considered with anything less than a 3.5 GPA (Grade Point Average). The mean GPA of medical student entrants is about 3.7, or three-tenths of a point away from a straight A average. In addition, applicants are required to take the MCAT (Medical College Admissions Test). Those accepted are usually in the eightieth percentile or above.

This makes sense. Before one can pass the board of medical examiners and become a licensed physician, he is required to study for many years. The training is intensive; and he is in competition with scores of other brilliant medical students. It takes a high IQ to keep up with the heavy intellectual demands. But this is only his initial training; it's only the beginning. During his internship he must study, conduct extensive research, and memorize a mind-boggling amount of facts and procedures. Then, throughout the years of his career, he must continue to study and learn in order to keep abreast of new developments in his profession. Although training may be rigorous and requirements stringent, it is imperative that a medical doctor be well-trained, highly intelligent and competent. Doctors can't afford to make serious mistakes!

Other professions also have certain standards and requirements. It's easy to see that a lame man can never make an Olympic runner. The stutterer will *not* do well as a lecturer. Impediments of these types are obvious. More obscure, and therefore less evident, are handicaps in the areas of aptitude, intelligence, and personality adjustment. Testing often eliminates those who can't make the grade. Yet, there are always some who slip through the screening processes and find themselves battling the odds in a job which does not suit their abilities. Tensions build up and tempers wear thin while round-pegged-people try in vain to fit into the square holes they have chosen.

I was invited to speak one day at the Central Intelligence Agency at our nation's Capitol. (The CIA is actually located in Virginia a few miles west of the Potomac River.) Naturally, I was excited about having this unusual opportunity. As we drove to the stately main building, I was extremely impressed with the beautiful grounds that surrounded it, but as the day unfolded, I was even more impressed with the high caliber people who were in the employ of this sophisticated organization. Later that afternoon, while talking with a man whose responsibility included the selection of personnel, I asked what procedures he followed to weed out less desirable applicants and to choose the best man for each job. He explained that the CIA administered certain qualifying exams to its applicants.

"What's more," he added, "we take a close look at an applicant's actual education, degrees and licenses. We want to be sure that the person we hire has enough in the upper story to function at a high level."

"How are these procedures working out?" I asked.

"Very well," he replied. "We take plenty of time and care in selecting the best qualified individual for each job, and as a result we don't have to make many changes."

How wise, I thought, for the CIA to use its "intelligence" to match the right person with the right job! No wonder there are not many changes of personnel. When an individual and his job are suited to each other, undesirable pressure is reduced to a minimum and one is free to perform at his maximum.

Ability and suitability, however, are not limited to the selective society of the professionals, or even to the CIA: they apply to everyone. Some jobs require less of some abilities and more of others. Although a beautician, for example, must have training at a beauty school, the process is not nearly as extensive or demanding as it is for someone who looks toward a career in engineering. To become a hairdresser, one not only needs a special interest in hair styling, but should like people and enjoy working with them personally; other abilities would include an artistic sense and manual dexterity. To be an engineer, however, one must have a bent for mathematics and the physical sciences. The engineer's creativity comes to light on the drawing board. The TV repairman, on the other hand, needs to have mechanical aptitude as well as interest and training in electronics. Without these qualities, I wouldn't want him working on *my* set.

Attitudes

Coupled with ability is another pressure indicator: Your attitude toward your work. It's very possible that you may have the necessary ability to handle a certain job, but not the interest. In that case, it's not for you. For example, a man may like to tinker around in his shop at home and do a little carpentry work in his spare time. It does not necessarily follow, however, that he would want to make it his vocation. Many times a person has enough ability to be quite successful in a certain field if he were to be so inclined, but the hitch is, he's not. Ability alone is not sufficient. If you are employed in a position where you do not have an interest in your work, you will *not* find your job satisfying, no matter how much ability you may have. Such a setup can only produce pressure.

Take the case of Jay, an accountant in a large business firm. Like others in that line of work, most of his working hours were spent indoors poring over books and figures. Jay, however, was not happy. Although he had no complaints about his salary—or his working conditions—or his associates, to him, each day was a frustrating grind. He considered the routine of an office as an intolerable bore: he did *not* enjoy his work. It wasn't that he was incapable of handling the position. On the contrary, Jay was trained and certainly had ability. His problem stemmed from a lack of *interest* in this kind of job. He disliked the confinement of an office. He wanted to be outside, involved with people. Instead, his job required isolation in a small room behind a desk. Jay felt boxed-in—like a prisoner. In his frustration there festered an underlying dissatisfaction, bringing with it tension and stress which carried over into his private life. This tension never eased until Jay changed his job for a related one which placed him outside of the office, allowing him more physical activity and contact with people. Jay still used his accounting background—but not behind four walls.

Boredom and distaste for a job, however, are not synonymous with pressure. Whereas pressure is the result of being insecure about one's ability to meet the demands of a given situation, boredom usually stems from a lack of stimulation. Boredom can create pressure, but it is not the pressure itself. For example, it would drive a college president to distraction if his job offered no more creative challenge or intellectual stimulation than those of a custodian. That's boredom. A custodian, on the other hand, might find himself with an emotional breakdown should he attempt to assume the role of the learned college president. That's pressure.

But boredom is easily converted into pressure. If, as in the case of the custodian and the college president, having too little or not the right kind of ability can put one under pressure, too much ability for a job can also be devastating. When your work offers no challenge, then boredom sets in. This, in turn, creates an emotional climate of frustration and dissatisfaction. Should this kind of turmoil continue to grow, it undoubtedly will show itself in the form of stress. Indeed, internal rankling or smoldering discontent, if not released or resolved, can build up into an intolerable pressure situation.

Boredom, which may seem innocent enough at first, is now exposed as a sinister pressure-producing agent. Of course, for the unmotivated or the indolent, it may seem to present a lesser evil, but for most people possessing the normal current of ambition and drive, boredom is not an acceptable state of being.

Unfortunately, there are comparatively few people who find their work exciting. . .or even very interesting. Many are bored because they have greater potential than their jobs allow. They are "stuck," however, because they have never developed their abilities and are unqualified to accept a more challenging opportunity. The world is filled with people who have not developed their talents.

Accountability

God holds us responsible for making the most of our abilities. The *amount* of our talent is not the issue: the *fact* is. In Matthew 25:14-30, Jesus tells the story of three servants whose master entrusted them with various talents: ". . .to one he gave five talents, to another two, and to another, one; every man according to his several ability. . ." (vs. 15). The servants with the *five* and the *two* both developed their talents to their fullest and the Lord commended them by saying that their work was "well done" and rewarded them for their faithfulness. But the servant with the measly little *one* talent did nothing about it. He just hid it in the ground and pretended that he had nothing for which he was accountable. But the Lord wasn't fooled, and the servant with "only" one talent was called to task for being "wicked" and slothful.

Actually, most of us aren't blessed with an abundance of talent. We aren't especially gifted. We aren't great artists, great musicians, great orators or great leaders. In fact, we aren't great anything. But does this let us off the hook? Does this mean we have no responsibilities? No, we all have at least *one* talent. Christ makes this clear in his illustration. And God holds us accountable for *any* ability He has placed in our hands. It's not up to us to judge its importance. God expects us to develop and use our talents, whether they are great—or very small!

If God has given you a mind with which to comprehend, then that in itself is a gift which should be used to aid in your personal growth. You owe it to God, who gave you the raw material, to cultivate it and develop it. God never intends for us to be second-rate. When we fight the odds of our own incompetence simply because we can't be bothered to put forth the effort to improve, we sin against God and ourselves. The resulting frustration can only produce pressure.

More Than Talent

The ability to perform a task well is seldom the sole result of a natural endowment. Even Mozart had to practice. Having the necessary training to develop your skills is both vital and necessary. It's as simple as this: If you have the proper know-how, you can tackle the job with ease, but if you struggle against incompetence, pressure can pile up like a mountain.

When lack of skill is the pressure-building culprit, it is usually possible to overcome this handicap by taking special training in the area of your need. Jan, for example, worked as a secretary for a hard-hitting executive. She was an excellent typist and she enjoyed doing letters and reports. Her shorthand, however, left room for improvement. It was definitely not up to par.

In Jan's particular job, however, shorthand was something she definitely needed. Because her boss had a habit of dictating in little snatches throughout the day, his dictation did not lend itself to electronic equipment. So Jan found herself uptight much of the time, worrying that she would not be able to get through the intermittent periods of dictation. The fact was, she usually didn't do too well and although her boss was patient, it was obvious that he was not pleased. Jan decided to do something about it before her boss did, so she signed up for an evening class in shorthand. In a semester's time she had improved tremendously. Now she was able to handle her boss's dictation with considerable ease. The extra training was enough to put Jan in the comfortable zone. She no longer felt she was walking on a threatening edge.

In recent years the emphasis on "how to" has produced a bumper crop of schools and classes of every description. Today, whether your need, like Jan's, is for greater secretarial skill, or whether your particular "thing" follows some other direction entirely, you have the opportunity to train in the area of your interest and need. There are day schools, night classes, private lessons, correspondence courses, seminars, summer training camps, and a host of other learning programs (many of them free) to say nothing of the millions of books on the market covering nearly every conceivable subject. If you really want to develop your potential, the opportunities are not beyond your reach.

Not For You

Although it is important to recognize your abilities and make the most of them, it is equally essential to be realistic about your limitations. Wishful thinking is a poor substitute for talent. Education helps but it is meant to develop, not be a stand-in, for God-given ability.

The story is told of a retarded farm boy who informed his elderly pastor that he felt God was calling him to the ministry.

"I had a vision," the simple lad told him, "and I saw two large letters—P.C. I'm sure that it must mean 'Preach Christ.' "

"Oh, no," the wise old pastor explained, "P.C. doesn't mean 'Preach Christ.' It means 'Plant corn.'"

I remember a classmate of mine in college. She was one of the most *un*musical persons I have ever met, and yet she was planning to be a music major. Everything she attempted in music was a major struggle. Unfortunately, it really wasn't worth the effort: the results were hard on the ear. One day I tactfully asked her why she had chosen to major in this field.

"Oh," she sweetly replied, "I've always wanted to marry an evangelist and travel with him as his pianist."

I don't know whether she had any particular "evangelist" in mind, but I doubted that she'd ever play the piano for anyone. Even lessons from Paderewski would not have transformed her into a musician!

By being realistic about our limitations, we can save ourselves a lot of grief. It is foolish and vain to pretend we have ability just because we wish we did, or because we want to impress others. While people might not catch on right away, they will eventually. The pressure of trying to live up to an image is destructive. How much better to be honest with ourselves—and others!

Many times our culture and our mores pressure us into feeling that we "ought to" do something that is really out of our line. We are made to believe that we "ought to" help out because we have been asked. If we decline, we are considered uncooperative and almost un-Christian. When we succumb to this kind of unwholesome motivation (even though our better judgment may be sending out warning signals) we often discover that by yielding to the pressure of a cultural "ought to," we have stepped into a much greater pressure trap.

Don't allow yourself to be pressured into positions that exceed your capability. Although there are situations in which we underestimate ourselves and need that extra push to get us started, there are other times when we *know* a job is beyond us. Elaine, the organist discussed earlier in this chapter, realized only too well that Handel's *Messiah* was out of reach for her musical capability. But, because of her strong sense of loyalty, she allowed the music committee to talk her into keeping her post as organist. She didn't want to "let the choir down" but in the end, not only did she pressure herself to the point of physical illness, but she was forced to do the very thing she was trying to avoid—she "let the choir down."

The Sunday school department of a certain church was in desperate need of a male teacher for a class of seventh-grade boys. When the superintendent approached Bob with the idea of teaching, he laughed out loud.

"Me, teach a class!" he guffawed, "Why, I've never taught in my life. Furthermore, I'm scared of kids—especially junior highers. I'd make a lousy teacher."

But the superintendent was "up a tree." He *had* to have someone for that class—so he put on the pressure—and at last Bob reluctantly gave in.

The class was a total fiasco. Spit wads and paper airplanes buzzed the room. Bob tried to teach some kind of a lesson but it was a lost cause. No one could hear him. He had no control of the class and had no idea how to get it. Even the "good kids" picked up the cues and began acting like rowdies.

By the close of that first Sunday school hour, Bob was ready to forget the whole mess. But again, pressure was applied for him to teach.

"Give it a long enough try, Bob," the superintendent told him. "Things will get better in a few weeks."

So Bob stayed on, but "things" didn't really get much better. He began to dread Sundays. By Saturday night his stomach was churning, and by Sunday noon he had a splitting headache to go with it. It was a horrible experience for Bob—and it didn't help the class much either.

Because we have been taught that it is our responsibility to help out when we are "needed," we sometimes find ourselves struggling over jobs which are packed with pressure. The same job to someone else might be "apple pie"—no strain, no pain.

Here's Sue, who entertains with dash and class as though it were nothing at all. It's not at all unusual for her to throw large dinner parties that would rival the courts of royalty for originality, atmosphere and delicious cuisine. Ann, on the other hand, has no flair along such lines. She dislikes cooking, and gets flustered just boiling an egg. Having one or two people over for a small luncheon throws her into a tizzy. It stands to reason that Ann is *not* the one to serve as chairman of the *hospitality committee*. But, for Sue, well, that's her cup of tea.

Especially for You

It is not God's intention that we should assume responsibilities which are outside the range of our abilities. He has equipped each individual with specific qualifications for specific purposes. God doesn't ask us to stand on our hands or write with our feet. Feet are made for standing and walking; hands for writing and many other accomplishments—but they are not for walking. Of course, there are a few circus acrobats who have trained themselves to walk on their hands but it's still no more than a stunt—and definitely not too efficient. The fact remains that the Lord plans for the members of our bodies to perform those tasks for which each was created. In the same way, we, too, have been endowed with individual gifts and talents.

God knows what He is doing when He gives people the wide variety of abilities that they share among themselves. It takes all of them in a cooperative effort to keep the wheels of our lives in smooth running order. This is also the way it is in the Christian life. The Apostle Paul explained it in his first letter to the Church at Corinth when he wrote: "Yes, the body has many parts, not just one part. . .He (God) has made many parts for our bodies and has put each part just where He wants it. . .All of you together are the one body of Christ and each one of you is a separate and necessary part of it. . . ."

Paul goes on to explain that we can't all be apostles, or prophets, or teachers or all of any one thing. Everyone has his own ability and is needed to fill his own individual assignment. When we are in the place that God has chosen for us, it is not only tailor-made to our individual abilities, but it is a place of personal satisfaction and peace.

33 READY AND ABLE

One day after a meeting where I'd been speaking, a lady said to me, "I think if I had your job I'd go crazy."

"Why is that?"

"Well," she said, "in the first place you're always speaking in public. And secondly, after you've spoken, people come up to talk to you and ask you for counsel."

I smiled and assured her that if I had to do her type of work I might find it a real chore too.

Who knows? Perhaps she was good at something else just as necessary as what I was doing.

Can we trust God, the author of our very potential, to arrange for a perfect marriage between our abilities and our responsibilities? Yes, but it doesn't come automatically. We need to be alert to our potential, realistic about our abilities, eager to improve, and sensitive to God's leading.

To be in His perfect will is to evoke the blessing of our Heavenly Father while avoiding the pitfalls of stress and pressure.

5. Loads and Limits

Thomas Edison once said, "I never did anything worth doing by accident, nor did any of my inventions come by accident; they came by work."

Don Herold expressed his feelings about work in satire. "Work," he said, "is the greatest thing in the world, so we should always save some of it for tomorrow."

A person's attitude toward work is a highly individual matter. If you were to check with work loads of a thousand people, you would find them as varied as the people themselves. Some go through life doing as *little* as possible. They're never especially interested or involved in accomplishment, but neither are they pressured by an overabundance of work. Others seem to perform in spurts: they show a spasmodic pattern of enthusiasm and industry, simmering down to disinterest and apathy, resulting, of course, in a fluctuating work output. Still others seem driven by a compulsion to do as much as they can, as fast as they can, as long as they can. Work is the story of their lives. While some seem barely able to drag through each "miserable" day, others keep looking for more hours in which to perform bigger and greater feats. Most of us hit it somewhere in between.

There are some who are highly motivated and unusually gifted. We recognize them as extremely capable and efficient persons with a high energy output. Their tremendous work performance is normal for them. They can handle a horrendous load, and thrive on it. There are others, however, who are saddled with a much-too-heavy work load, without this positive, motivating force. They don't stick with it because they find the work so challenging and exciting, but because they have no choice. They have a problem of the income being incompatible with the outgo. And so they are compelled to work hard and long in order to meet financial obligations. It is easy to understand why they feel trapped. There are others, however, who carry weighty work loads without legitimate motivation. In such cases, the dynamics producing the flurry of perpetual activity are unhealthy and undesirable. The end product is invariably tension and emotional stress.

For most people, *work* is not a popular concept. The idea of play, relaxation, vacation—or just plain rest—lights up the eyes and elicits smiles. These are the things that you enjoy—something you *want* to do. But with work, there is no option: it must be done. In Mark Twain's American masterpiece, *Tom Sawyer*, he explains that "Work consists of whatever a body is not obliged to do." This, of course, is an oversimplification but it does point out the importance of one's attitude toward the things he does.

The celebrated English critic, John Ruskin, is reported to have said, "In order for people to be happy in their work, these three things are needed: They must be fit for it; *They must not have too much of it*; And they must have a sense of success in it." Although all three of these elements are vital, it is possible that a person may be "fit" for his work, and may feel that necessary "sense of success" but still find work a drag because there's "too much of it." We've all experienced the pressure of work pileups. The human organism can cope with work surges as long as the wave of work isn't too overwhelming or last excessively long. But when "overwork" becomes the pattern day in and day out, one's mind and body will eventually rebel.

They Work Too Hard

If overwork kills the enjoyment of work and exerts destructive pressures, why do people become slaves to it? What are the impelling motivations forcing free human beings into a work-work-work syndrome? There are numerous reasons, some obvious, but many are subtle and disguised. People who are "workaholics" seldom understand the dynamics which prompt them to place work in such an unhealthy perspective.

Some people are victims of circumstances. They are trapped. They have no choice but to accept the pressures of heavy work loads because there's no other way out. Here's Joe, the sole breadwinner for his family of eight. He and his wife have five children, and in addition, Joe has the care of his wife's aged, invalid mother who lives with the family. Joe's education terminated with tenth grade when his father died and it was necessary for him to get a job to help out the family. He never was much of a student so it never occurred to him to go back to school and get his high school diploma. Naturally, because of his low educational status, he was unqualified for anything except a low-paying job. After his marriage, and the responsibilities of a growing family, expenses mounted beyond his meager income. To meet the necessities of life, Joe found that he must "moonlight" by taking on other jobs on weekends and evenings. His work was hard and his hours were long, but there was nothing he could do about it.

There are people like Joe who are caught in a web beyond their control, but for most of us it is a different story. There are many "moonlighters" and overtime employees who really wouldn't need to work that hard if they were willing to do without some of the luxuries and frills of our highly developed civilization. Of course, working for a goal is legitimate, and often commendable, but not at the expense of our well-being. If the pressure of overwork is taking its toll on our personal happiness and relationships with others, it's time to take inventory of our values. Are we sacrificing our health and happiness for the sake of status? Do we really need those technological gadgets? Is it pride that prods us to keep up with the Joneses? Or is it greed that is driving us to workaholism?

We may think we're in a trap, but more times than not, the lock is on the inside and we hold the key ourselves. Perhaps in your job your boss expects the impossible. He piles on more work than it is humanly possible to accomplish within the hours of your working day. The only alternative, as you see it, is to stay late at the office or take work home with you at night. You soon discover that you have round-the-clock employment, which leaves no time to tend to personal affairs or to relax. You chafe under these conditions but you rationalize by telling yourself that the job pays well, and you can't afford to accept a lower salary. The question is, can you afford to continue as you are? What good is the money if getting it means giving up your personal identity? Wouldn't you be better off taking a job with less prestige and less pay than to stay where you are ruining your health and disposition?

Stressful situations, however, are not necessarily brought on by insensitive employers. The success seeker—whether in business or a profession—is often a glutton for choosing pressure-packed options. With responsibilities weighing heavily upon him, the eager beaver pushes himself to the breaking point trying to achieve the bigger and the better. Ulcers are accepted as an occupational hazard. He seems to be unaware that when the demands of a job consume all of a person's time and energy, his losses are greater than his gains. In his attempt to climb to the top, he has become a stranger in his own household, and, of course, he's either too busy or too tired to attend church. In other words, he no longer has time for God and he is too busy for his family. What a price to pay for "success!" Without the sustaining power of God and the heartwarming support of loved ones, the pressures of business must be carried alone. Is it worth it?

Sometimes we push ourselves too hard because we have an exalted opinion of our own importance. We are positive that we are indispensable and that the world could not get along without us. Of course, if we push hard enough, sooner or later we'll reach the breaking point and discover the startling truth: we are *not* indispensable after all. We just thought we were.

Trying to live up to an image is no small task. It places demands upon one that can only lead to pressure. A woman, for example, may feel that she is not fulfilling her role as wife and mother unless she bakes homemade bread, sews her families' wardrobe, keeps a spotless house, participates in PTA activities, attends a flower arranging class, is den mother for the cub scouts and goes to the gym twice a week to keep herself slim and trim. "Hectic" is the word describing such a schedule. The truth of the matter is she could be a much better wife and mother if she were not so busy. In breathlessly dashing from one activity to another, she becomes harried and pressured. This causes her to be "uptight" and nervous—which, in turn, affects the atmosphere of the home and relationships within the family. The measure of a good wife or a good mother is not calculated so much by the number of things she does as in her warmth and loving acceptance of her family. This is not to say that a homemaker isn't busy. If you are a homemaker, you are all too aware of the countless demands on your time. But you can't do everything suggested by TV commercials and magazine ads. And your mother-in-law was *not* superwoman, even if your husband seems to think she was. Trying to do *everything* will tie you up in knots, and it's hard on the marriage knot as well.

Another "busy bee" who buzzes himself to distraction is the *perfectionist*. He works and works to have everything just right and is upset if things aren't exactly the way he thinks they ought to be. But since he lives in an imperfect world populated with imperfect people, this poses a problem. Nevertheless, he continues to do his "part," as he sees it, working harder and harder to achieve his ideal. Although people need a standard of excellence and have an obligation to work to the best of their ability, the perfectionist goes beyond this. He is never satisfied. His days are filled with frustrations. And since he expends his time and energy fussing over picayune details, it takes much longer to get the job done.

Reasons or Excuses?

There are many varieties of "workaholics," and most of them attempt to rationalize their position. "We're trying to save money," some say as they attempt all kinds of home and other ambitious projects. This is fine if you can handle it without undue stress. However, there's no virtue in being a do-it-yourself technician if doing it yourself brings with it a wave of unwarranted pressure.

Others explain that "there's so much to do but no one else to do it." This could mean that these individuals are being imposed upon by inconsiderate persons such as family members, friends, or employers. Or it could mean that they are doing more than they are expected to do. In either case, when work reaches the proportions of strain and hardship, it's time that a person have enough self-esteem to stand up for his rights. In a pleasant way, explain that you can no longer be responsible for as much work as you have been doing. Others, engrossed in their own affairs, may be totally unaware that you have been straining under a heavy load. You owe it to yourself and to the others involved to let them know.

You've Never Learned to Say "No"

In many areas of the world, the gawky camel is the principal beast of burden. Although this strange animal may not look too intelligent, he is known to be quite discriminating when it comes to the weight of the load he carries. It seems as though he will take so much—but not a bit more. If his master should try to exceed his limits, he balks and stubbornly refuses to budge until the load is lightened.

Although a camel knows his limits, it is apparent that many human beings do not. (Could it be that, in this respect, the lowly camel is actually superior to his master?) Although "no" is usually the first word a toddler learns to say—and exercises the use of it most frequently, it would seem that as people grow into adulthood, they forget the use of it. At least, there are great numbers who have never learned to say "no."

Have you ever wondered why you are such a "sucker"? Why *do* you accept added responsibilities when you've already got more to do than you know how to get done? Is your sales-resistance low? If so, why? Let's check the directives—the underlying motivations which could predispose you to take on more than you ought to be doing:

1. *You don't know your own limits*. Are you realistic about your strengths and your limitations? There are those who are highly creative and ambitious. They are spirited people who thrill to a challenge and like to get in the action. Unfortunately, their physical and/or emotional stamina may not match their

gregarious personalities. Because the "want to" is so strong, they tend to minimize their limitations, but in time they must deal with the consequences. All of us have limits. No one is superman. It's a wise person who has learned the limits of his endurance.

2. *You want people to like you*. There are many who suffer from a basic feeling of insecurity and lack of worth—undoubtedly, fostered by emotional deprivations and negative experiences in childhood. They have learned that by *doing* for other people, they can build up Brownie points and thereby gain a certain measure of acceptance. In severe cases, people will literally work themselves to death in an attempt to buy the approval of others. This kind of addiction to work is a bid for recognition. If you feel you must "do" for other people in order for people to like you, you are suffering from a low self-image and need to explore the dynamics of your problem with a qualified counselor.

3. *It's part of your culture*. Perhaps you were brought up that way. How many times do parents tell their youngsters, "When we ask you to do something, *do it!*"? We teach our children to be obliging and to help out when there is a need. This, of course, is right: children need to be made aware of responsibility. Adults, however, must determine priorities and decline involvement in those which are not. It's fine to be a good guy who likes to help people, but when these extra responsibilities produce undue stress and strain, perhaps your activities need a priority evaluation.

The Impossible Dream

Some people set goals for themselves that are completely out of reach—no matter how much they stretch. In attempting the impossible, they strive and strain and struggle, but all they get is stress. Furthermore, these people will never achieve their goals because the goals are unrealistic and impractical. Sure, I've heard about Wilbur and Orville Wright. . .and a few other courageous individuals like them. But we're discussing a different matter. We are speaking of people who have hitched their wagon to a star that isn't there.

For the most part, those who toil and struggle after unrealistic goals are making a subconscious attempt to supply basic emotional needs which were never met in childhood—perhaps feelings of belonging, of being worthwhile, or being loved. So they go through life working longer, harder, climbing higher, always striving to find acceptance. Unfortunately, they are reaching for a mirage. Acceptance is not a by-product of accomplishment. Rather, it is established through relationships.

I remember an experience I had while working on my doctorate at Columbia University. A fellow student and I were discussing our studies when suddenly in the middle of the conversation he remarked, "Do you know why I think I am getting my doctor's degree?"

"Why?" I asked.

"To please my dad. My dad never complimented me. I've spent years of my life and used up my money trying to get this doctor's degree and I still don't have it." Then, wistfully he asked, "Do other people do things like that?"

"You know," he continued, "at times I've actually dreamed that I finished my doctoral requirement and went home with my degree. In my dream my father was very proud and happy. . .and he *hugged* me." After a moment's thoughtful pause he added, "But even if I ever do get my doctor's degree and go home with my sheepskin, he still won't compliment me, will he? He's never done it before. Dad's a smart man and a good man, but he doesn't compliment anyone. Actually, I guess I'm just knocking my brains out for nothing."

If you are reaching for the "impossible dream," check yourself for motives. What are you trying to prove? Are you "knocking yourself out" to impress others and thereby gain status? Or might it be an attempt to compensate for basic emotional needs that lacked the nurture of a fulfilling childhood? If you are building your case on any of the above motivations, you are building on a wrong premise. Yet you need not give up hope or feel discouraged because you are loved and accepted by your Heavenly Father. He loves you just the way you are, and no amount of working or striving will increase or decrease His love for you. It matters not to God whether you are on the lowest or the highest rung of the educational, social, or economic ladder—or somewhere in between. He loves you because He has chosen to love you—just the way you are.

A Form of Hostility

Overwork has many overtones. One that is seldom recognized, however, is that it may actually be a form of hostility.

Everyone knew that Trudy was a hard worker. Not only was she a busy homemaker, with a husband and three children to care for, but she held a demanding job in a downtown realtor's office. Her husband had preferred that she did not work outside the home, but Trudy insisted that she wanted to "help out." On weekends and evenings Trudy was busy wallpapering the dining room, painting the den, reupholstering the divan, sewing, cleaning, baking, remodeling, washing, ironing, scrubbing, ad infinitum. She was never idle a moment. Even on those rare occasions when she sat and watched TV her fingers bobbed back and forth with knitting needles as she worked away on another project. Although people admired Trudy for her tremendous industry, very few felt they knew her. She was always too busy for "socializing." She lived in a cloud of self-made pressure.

Trudy's compulsion to work was not the result of a financial need. Her husband made an adequate salary, and would have gladly hired others to do many of the jobs she tackled herself. He often pled with her not to drive herself so hard, but to no avail. Indeed, Trudy had no intention of slackening her pace.

Although Trudy didn't know it, and others may not have realized it, she was an extremely hostile person. Orphaned as a young child, Trudy was raised by an aunt and uncle with whom she had little or no positive relationships. When they would scold or berate her, Trudy learned to control her anger and frustration by turning to work. She would vigorously sweep, or scrub, or do something else while she fought back the tears, kept her silence, and pitied herself. Today, as a grown woman with her own family, she harbors feelings of hostility and resentment, but by working hard, she senses a measure of relief. Subconsciously, she still wants to pity herself, so by overworking, she can inwardly claim the role of a martyr.

Hostility vented in the form of overwork can be directed either inwardly or outwardly. In other words, it might represent a self-punitive measure in which you inflict the suffering of overwork on yourself because you feel unworthy and inadequate, deserving only of punishment. On the other hand, it could be used as a weapon to humble and shame others, because you have to work so very, very hard. In one instance, your anger is aimed towards yourself. When directed toward others, your heavy work load is used as an opportunity to get even and to make others feel guilty because you are so overworked. In other words, you have become a martyr, and for some reason, you'd like them to feel that it's all their fault.

There are many like Trudy who unknowingly punish themselves and others by overworking. They don't feel deserving unless they are continually working. As children they were never made to feel acceptable the way they were. In order to gain love—or simply approval—they had to do, do, do! Now as adults they are still "doing." They are seldom aware of the dynamics motivating their drive for perpetually being busy. There are many men and women who stretch themselves far beyond the normal; pushing relentlessly, morning, noon and night. They find it difficult to sit down and relax or to play a game or just lounge around. They have to be doing something. Deep down inside, they feel that unless they are "doing" they will not be loved, accepted or respected by others. And so the internal drive pushes them on.

You need to ask yourself, "Why am I working so hard? Am I trying to prove something to myself or to someone else? Is this my way of getting even? Or am I looking for acceptance? Perhaps I'm trying to please somebody back in my childhood? Or am I trying to accept myself by 'doing' more and more?"

Eager Beaver

There are a few human dynamos who thrive on work loads that would stagger the average person. They have an insatiable drive for accomplishment and have disciplined themselves to make every moment count. Geniuses and near geniuses are often in this category. Thomas Edison was this kind of a man. He was an avid worker and took little interest in anything other than his work. This remarkable man is credited with having patented over one thousand inventions, many of which are indispensable in our modern way of life. Albert Einstein was another tireless worker. His work, which opened the door for space travel, enveloped his life. But most of us aren't Einsteins or Edisons. These are the exception, not the rule.

Although some may find it hard to believe, there are those who thoroughly enjoy their work and love to do it for the sheer sake of accomplishment. Endowed with an abundant share of drive and ambition, heavy work loads do not take the form of pressure, but are thought of as stimulating challenges. There is a danger, however, that because of the intensity of involvement and excitement of accomplishment, these people may not recognize the pressure of overwork. This is also true of people who feel a strong sense of urgency about their work, such as ministers, missionaries or crusaders for a specific cause. But the gifted and the dedicated are as vulnerable as anyone else, and the strenuous pace of continual overwork is bound to take its toll. It is often true that family members and close friends are concerned because they realize that their loved one (or friend) is working too hard, expending himself without reserve. They may recognize the symptoms of stress before the victim is aware of it.

The Origin of Work

Many times we forget that God is the originator of work. In case this causes you to feel hostile towards God, let's examine the subject further.

44
HOW TO HANDLE PRESSURE

The very first words of the Bible, Genesis 1:1, tell us that "in the beginning, God created the heavens and the earth." That's a big order! That's work of staggering proportions, but it's the kind of work God was involved in. Yes, God was and still is a worker. And when He created man, God created him in His own likeness and placed in Adam an innate ability and a will to work.

Adam was given his work detail by God Himself—an assignment which included tending and caring for the magnificent Garden of Eden. He was also put in charge of all the animals, and given the Gargantuan task of naming them. But none of this work could be considered as undesirable. It was a challenge and a responsibility that resulted in the joy of accomplishment. A sense of accomplishment is fundamental to our basic human make up. For Adam, this found fulfillment in the work responsibility which God entrusted to him.

Work, in its original context, was divinely inspired and noble. It was a creative exercise and a rewarding experience. It provided a unique outlet for one's abilities and talents—a very important function of work. And in its completion it offered a fulfillment and a pleasure that comes only from the satisfaction of a job well done. This is not vanity or conceit. It is a divine characteristic: God Himself reviewed each creative day and "saw that it was good."

God, however, never intended work to be an all-consuming passion. If He had, He never would have rested on the seventh day. God wasn't tired. God did not rest because of His own inadequacies, but because He wanted to give work its proper value. Accomplishment is not everything. Our relationship to God takes priority over all other responsibilities as illustrated on the seventh or Sabbath day when work was set aside for worship. Worship, however, is not a one-day-a-week affair. Man was made to worship every day, but work is eliminated on the Sabbath to show its proper perspective in God's divine plan.

But work, as we know it, is a "horse of a different color." It has lost its original luster. It is taxing and tiring. More times than not, it is sheer drudgery, demanding and destroying the best of ourselves. Why? What happened to the original work plan?

When sin brought its somber fate upon man and the planet on which he had been placed, the status of human work received a crushing blow. Removed from its elevated position of "creative challenge," work became a struggle for existence. Ever since the fall of man, work, hard hit by the curse, has represented "toil" by means of "the sweat of the brow." Although man is still capable of fantastic accomplishments, his inspiration is almost always diffused with perspiration. Work, for the most part, is no longer an experience of joy and delight. To many, it is merely a "necessary evil." It becomes the old grind that one does because he has no alternative.

When the Burden is Light

Work itself is not pressure. The pressure part comes when more is demanded than can be produced without undue effort. Take a machine, for example. For a smooth, trouble-free performance, it should be used, but not abused. This means that: (1) its mechanism should be properly suited to the task to be accomplished, and (2) it should primarily operate at the level of its greatest efficiency. Suppose you have a small sports car. Were you to habitually drive it over rough terrain as you might a jeep, or use it for cross-country hauling of heavy refrigerators, your car would be heading for a breakdown. It wasn't intended for such usage.

People, of course, aren't machines, but many are much more demanding of themselves than they are of gadgets made of nuts and bolts and metal parts. They struggle along trying to hold down jobs for which they have no natural inclination or lack insufficient training or experience. Sometimes, however, a person can learn as he goes along, and thereby overcome his handicap by adapting himself to the job. By accepting the challenge, he actually stretches himself to increased capabilities. The ability to "grow" is probably man's greatest advantage over the "machine." But undue pressure will stunt growth and is unhealthy.

The most common producer of work pressure today is simply too much of it. We require ourselves to "produce beyond our God-given limits." We try to do more than God intends for us to do.

Let's refer again to machinery: We know that construction and purpose dictate the limits of a load. For maximum efficiency, a machine cannot consistently maintain a load that exceeds the one recommended by the manufacturer. It was designed to carry a certain amount. To take less is not utilizing its full capacity. To weight it down with more is asking for trouble. For awhile it may seem as though the manufacturer has underestimated the strength and durability of his product. Nevertheless, the overload takes its toll. It imposes stresses and strains upon the mechanism which it was never intended to sustain. The result: parts wear down and the general efficiency of the machine decreases. In time, it becomes noisy and no longer runs as fast or as smoothly as it once did. It may even break down completely.

We have seen how machinery is limited by its designer and manufacturer. In a divine sense, God—the master designer and creator of mankind—also places limits upon every one of us. These limits vary with each individual matching his need, his ability, and his strength. God has a plan and purpose for every life. When we operate within the framework of His design, our lives are characterized by peace and joy. We are not pressured because the amount we have to do does not exceed God's will for our lives. His plan does not assign work details that crowd our schedules to the point of strained relationships and emotional or physical exhaustion. When the load you're carrying creates pressure and stress, you're either deviating from God's purpose or exceeding His limits for you.

When too many responsibilities crowd around you, they become burdens. When there are more demands on your time than you have hours in the day, the pressure weighs heavier and heavier. You are weary, not only from all your labors, but from the weight of all that there is still left to do. Jesus is concerned about people's work loads. In Matthew 11:28-30, He lovingly reaches forth a helping hand to those of us who are work worn and "heavy laden" with the demands of living. Jesus offers Himself as the solution to our pressure problems in a message of love and hope: He tells us, "Come unto me, all ye that labor and are heavy laden, and I will give you rest" (Matthew 11:28).

"Come." That's the only requirement, but it's an essential. You must take the step of faith and God will do the rest. To "come" means to meet God with your need, to acknowledge your sin and your helplessness, and accept His Son as your personal Savior. This is the initial step, but a crucial one.

Unfortunately, there are many who, although they have taken that first step, are still "heavy laden," and pressured. They're still struggling with the problem of too much to do and not enough time in which to do it. What's wrong? Sure they belong to the Lord, but when it comes to rest, they are waiting until the millennium. It's obvious that there's no time to rest with their schedules the way they are.

But the promise of giving rest to workworn people who spend time with Jesus still stands. Those who bring their pressures and burdens to Him find that He lifts pressures and eases burdens. They are revived and refreshed—yes, rested, because they have come to Jesus. This, of course, must be on a daily basis. Every day as you come to Jesus, He offers strength for the day. To neglect this power source is like going to battle without weapons and ammunition. You are unprepared to face the foe. So it is in our daily lives. We make ourselves vulnerable to stresses and tensions of all descriptions when we aren't prepared to handle them.

When Jesus promises rest to those who come to Him, He is not referring to an extended vacation or a retirement plan. It is not God's plan or purpose to minimize the importance of work or deprive us of the joy of accomplishment. On the contrary, Jesus emphasizes the urgency of work, when He told His disciples, "I must work the works of Him that sent me, while it is day: the night cometh when no man can work" (John 9:4).

It's not difficult to reconcile working and resting, because one is meant to follow the other. Christ offers rest to those who labor and are heavy laden, or under strain and pressures. Those who accept His offer are revived and refreshed. With renewed strength and vigor they are ready to tackle the job He has mapped out for them because they are not doing it alone. "Take my yoke upon you," Jesus says in Matthew 11:29, "and learn of me." When we take Christ's yoke upon us (note that we align ourselves with Christ—*not* He with us) we no longer work alone. Christ is working by our side: He's then pulling with us, helping us through the rough places. What a pressure lifter! Yet, that is not all. Not only is He helping us bear the load but He is teaching us. "On the job training," you might call it. And as we learn of Him, we discover the greatness of God's love and power. He patiently guides our steps along the right paths and keeps us from making mistakes. He lovingly shows us our weaknesses, and how we can have His strength. Our work is to be a learning process which will help us depend upon our Lord and come to know Him better.

Are you in the kind of work where God can teach you to rely on Him? Is Jesus your senior partner on the job, in the classroom, or as you perform your duties at home—and are you learning from Him and about Him in all that you do? This is the way it has to be. This is God's plan for your life and for mine. If you are in a position where Christ cannot work with you and where you are hindered from *learning of Him*, you are not where God wants you to be. You cannot claim the promise of God's rest if you are not in God's place for you.

Actually, God's Word says that when we have aligned ourselves with Christ and become His apprentice, we continue to rid ourselves of a great deal of pressure as we grow spiritually and become more and more like Him. In the last half of Matthew 11:29 (the verse we have been discussing) Jesus goes on to explain, "for I am meek and lowly of heart and ye shall find rest unto your souls." *Meek and lowly of heart*. That doesn't sound like today's highly competitive society! We push, we shove, we hurry, we rush so that we can be first—or the biggest—or the best. When we *learn of Him* and become more "meek and lowly of heart" we learn to see things in their proper perspectives. We won't feel the need for "keeping up with the Joneses." We'll understand God's viewpoint and see how the first shall be last and the last shall be first. Then, as our feverish activities of self-aggrandizement give way to the meek and lowly spirit of Christ, we shall find rest unto our souls. A Christlike spirit is not a pressured one.

Christ sums up His offer in these words: "For my yoke is easy and my burden light" (Matthew 11:30). Yes, when we are in the harness with Christ, we are not overworked. His yoke is *easy*. His burden is light. There's no undue stress or tension coming from a harried routine or too heavy a load.

We may think that what we are doing is the Lord's work—but if the race and the pace leave you in a cloud of pressure, then you've taken things in your own hands. Jesus said, "My yoke is *easy*. . .My burden is *light*." To assume a heavier load than God intends for you is presumptuous. The pressure you feel is a warning that you've overstepped your bounds.

6 · The Drag of Distractions

Keith Williams settled back on the 5:15 commuter train, glad to be going home after a grueling day at the office. Tired and frustrated, he began a mental recount of the day's activities.

It had been a busy day all right! There had been meetings to attend, unannounced visitors and a misunderstanding to straighten out between two fellow employees. That took the morning. A luncheon engagement with a prospective buyer took more than the usual forty-five minute midday break. Adding to the confusion was the fact that Keith's secretary had taken the afternoon off for personal business. Hunting for needed materials was a time-consuming process: he never could figure out her system of filing. To top it off, the telephone seemed to be on a rampage. Among the many phone interruptions were four calls from Keith's wife asking what to do about a problem with her car.

It had been a hectic day indeed! Even worse, it had been one of frustration. Very little of Keith's regular work had been accomplished. He hadn't even glanced at the day's correspondence. Tomorrow could easily find him in a bind, because of today's leftover work. It made him feel pressured just thinking about it.

Fortunately for Keith Williams, this had not been a typical day. Most of the time he was able to keep up with his work at least reasonably well. Of course, there were some days—like this one—that were hard to come by.

"I don't mind the work," Keith shared with his wife that evening, "It's those interruptions all day long that drive me up a wall. I can't get my work done under conditions like that."

50
HOW TO HANDLE PRESSURE

The Day That Got Away

There are many who belabor a continual drag of distractions. For them, life is a series of interruptions. Coping with the unexpected becomes an accepted way of life. It isn't easy, but that's the way it is.

Not among the least of these is the harried mother of assorted age children. Take, for example, Fran, the mother of four. The day starts off in its inimitable fashion when six-year-old Susie chokes over a piece of toast (she had too big a mouthful) and ends up vomiting over her clean dress, the table, and the floor. Mom to the rescue. Beginning with Susie who needs tears wiped and a whole set of clean clothing, mother cleans up the mess. By now, Susie has missed the school bus. The only alternative is to chuck the two pajama-clad younger children into the car along with Susie and drive her to school. Fran's the chauffeur, of course.

Home again, Fran begins her daily routine of household chores. For an hour or so there are no more than the usual amount of interruptions—like a phone call from her mother-in-law, the Fuller Brush man at the door, and a squabble or two to settle between the kids.

Then a neighbor, poking her head in the side door, informs Fran that she has seen their dog running down the street. The meter man, Fran discovers, has failed to close the gate. The neighbor generously offers to stay with the "baby" (a one-and-a-half-year-old boy) while Fran and her four-year-old daughter drive up and down the neighborhood streets, intermittently whistling and calling the name of their mongrel pet. After a futile search, the two return home while Fran vainly attempts to comfort the worried and tearful little girl snuggled in the seat beside her.

Just as they pull up in front of their house, the child lets out a squeal of delight, for there is "Poochie" across the street, blithely playing a game of chase with a large stray dog on a freshly seeded lawn.

The baby-sitting neighbor is glad they have found Poochie. She says she has enjoyed staying with the baby, and from the looks of the toys strewn all over the floor, baby has enjoyed it, too. Fran thanks her and asks if she would like a cup of coffee. The neighbor, whose only child is in junior high, sits around for almost an hour sipping coffee and telling about her "do-it-yourself" exploits. When the kids begin whimpering for their overdue lunch, Fran's friendly neighbor finally takes the hint and goes home.

Except for a broken jelly jar (the result of her "helpful" preschooler) lunch time is relatively calm and uneventful. Fran cleans up the mess of intermingled jelly and glass and begins the process of getting her little ones ready for their nap. She is really looking forward to nap time. This is when Fran plans on getting things done.

51
THE DRAG OF DISTRACTIONS

Suddenly a bloodcurdling scream resounds through the house. Fran races to the kitchen (the source of the disturbing sound) and lifts a bloodsmeared little boy from the floor. An examination of the wailing toddler reveals a nasty cut on his left hand. A piece of broken glass which Fran had missed from the jelly jar episode had unfortunately *not* been missed by Junior. Naps become secondary as Fran and her little ones head for the pediatrician. Three stitches are needed on the plump little hand.

Hurrying home, our heroic mother manages to arrive just a few minutes before the two older children, Susie and Scot, get home from school. After a snack, Scot, who is nine, informs his mother that the gears are broken on his bicycle. Since it's too far to walk, this means that Fran must pile the kids in the car and drive Scot to and from his piano lesson. After the lesson she stops at the market to buy some groceries, then heads on home to start preparations for dinner.

When Hubby comes home, he's not going to rate high on his wife's popularity scale if he makes disparaging remarks or asks insensitive questions like "What do you *do* with yourself all day?"—"It must be nice to stay home and not have to work."—"How come the house is so messy? You've got the whole day to clean it up." That's what she *doesn't* need.

Later that evening, after the children are all tucked in bed and asleep, Fran flops into an easy chair, exhausted. "What in the world?" she ponders, "I've sure been busy today, but what have I got to show for it? I didn't get any of the things done that I had planned and yet, here I am just *bushed*!"

Of course, not every day turns out to be as demanding as this one has been. But then again, sometimes it's worse. "At least," Fran mused, "I wasn't expecting guests home for dinner tonight."

It's sheer frustration to feel as though you've worn yourself to a frazzle just marking time—especially when you've got somewhere to go. Most healthy people set up goals for accomplishment. If you work for someone else, your employer will set the goals for you. In either case they may be short term or immediate goals, or they may be long-ranged. Most of us have a combination of both.

But goals are not always that easy to achieve—not because of their difficulty, but because of distractions and interruptions which interfere with performance. When you're working in a situation that demands a deadline (and who doesn't?) these interferences can impede your progress to the point of causing immeasurable pressure.

Since no one lives in a vacuum, no one can ever be completely free from distractive influences. In fact, many times they serve a helpful purpose by offering a diversion when one is needed. But when interruptions and other distractions slow you down until you feel tense and nervous because you are so far behind in your work, it's time to take action and protect yourself from unnecessary interference.

What Shall I Do?

First of all, evaluate your priorities. It could even be that the interruption is more important than the project. Suppose you are busily working on an important report when someone breaks into your privacy and shouts, "The building is on fire. Evacuate the premises." Would you resent the messenger's intrusion? And would you argue that you'd have to stay because your report was due in the morning and if you hoped to finish it, you'd have to keep right at it? I should say not! Any person in his right mind would leave a burning building at once—no questions asked. The report? Oh sure, it's important—but not as important as your life.

Other priorities may not be as spectacular as this, but they must also be viewed with the proper perspective. A mother may set goals for herself to redecorate the home or do a certain amount of entertaining, but if her children need more of her attention, they are her first responsibility. Fran, the mother of four discussed earlier, felt at the end of the day as though she had not accomplished much. Actually, she had fulfilled the requirements of a high priority: she had cared for the needs of her children.

Fathers must face this priority as well. As a father, you may be a good "provider" of temporal needs, but when you become so involved with making money that family matters are considered as "interruptions," it's time to examine your priorities. The truth of the matter may be that your job is distracting you from the important business of being the husband and father that God intends you to be.

Sorting out priorities can be a good pressure releaser. When you face the facts that no job, no matter how important, supersedes your relationships to God and your family, much of your tension and stress may be resolved. Some things that have seemed vitally important to you before may shift their positions to lower levels of value.

When you are sure that your priorities are in proper place, it's up to you to protect those priorities from destructive forces of distraction. When you work in an office, a shop, or in some other place of business, your employer often protects you from too many interruptions or disturbance factors; since you are on his payroll, he wants to insure your efficiency. Lengthy personal conversations are frowned upon. You are paid to get the job done, not socialize. When other distractions interfere with your work output (such as handling too many telephone calls or unexpected side issues), it is best to discuss it with your superior and find out what his priorities are for you on your job. If he wants you to continue with all these "extras," then you need not consider them as pressure, but as priorities. If he feels that these "extras" interfere with what he considers a better use of your time, it is up to him to solve the problem. If you have adequately explained the situation to your employer, then the concern is his, not yours.

On work where you are responsible for controlling your own distraction, the solution may not be so simple. Often this problem proves especially troublesome if your work is carried on in or near your home. Unless you live alone, when your home base is used for an office, a studio or a shop, you are vulnerable by reason of being available. When you are too available, you are likely to have family members and friends popping in to see you at any time. If you are working on something that demands concentration, a steady stream of friendly well-wishers can be extremely disruptive. This is especially true of work that requires originality. Indeed, interruptions are lethal to creative thought. Furthermore, you cannot expect others to buy the idea that what you are *doing* is any more important than what they have to *say*.

The conflict between your availability and your desired isolation can become a sticky issue. . .but it doesn't need to. Try quietly and patiently explaining to your wife, children, great-aunt Phoebe, next door neighbor, mother-in-law, or whoever else frequents your working domain, that, except for extreme emergencies, you must not be disturbed when in your office or studio, or between certain predetermined hours of the day. After all, if you were working somewhere else, they wouldn't be able to be with you either. Let them know, however, that you are eager to talk with them when you are not working. Then be sure to keep your part of the agreement.

But you must be reasonable. You can't decide to settle yourself in the middle of the living room or spread your work across the dining room table and expect the rest of the family to tiptoe through the house behaving like a tribe of mutes. That would be selfish and inconsiderate. A home is for living. If you insist upon staying in the middle of the activity area, you aren't really serious about eliminating distractions. When it shows up in your work, you'll suffer the consequences, but there will be no one to blame but yourself.

This is a common struggle among students. Johnny does his homework in the family room—within earshot of the TV, of course. In this way he can keep up on the latest sports news—while his grades, incidentally, go down. Then there's the University coed whose room is the social center of the dorm. Naturally she enjoys the popularity, but it makes it hard to keep up with her studies. If she really wants to concentrate, she had better absent herself to the confines of the library. Some collegians find it difficult to get much accomplished because of talkative roommates. The library is often the answer to this problem too—or even a switch in roommates.

Bell: A Burden or a Blessing?

What about the telephone?

It has been said that Alexander Graham Bell, the indomitable inventor of that instrument, has bequeathed to modern civilization one of its greatest assets.

Most would endorse this statement. There are others, however, who recognize that the telephone also brings with it some serious liabilities. Whereas, the phone has made life easier for the majority, there are some for whom it has produced a pileup of pressure.

A hard-hitting business man surprised his friends and neighbors when he pulled up stakes from his suburban community and moved his family to a sparsely settled rural area. When asked about phone service, he replied, "I'm not going to have any. That's one of the reasons I'm moving to the country—so I won't be bothered by salesmen and the telephone!" He wanted to get away from it all.

It is true that a telephone can be extremely demanding. Although it can be a blessing, it can also be a big bother. When your phone rings almost incessantly, disturbs you when you should be left alone, interferes with your routine, and pressures you to the point of distraction, Bell's invention has become a burdensome intruder.

Of course, for some people the telephone presents no problem. They don't receive many calls and welcome each one as a relief from their isolation. Others, however, tell a different story. Their work or their life-style predisposes the phone to ring almost day and night. Besides disrupting their privacy, they are often hampered in being able to get much accomplished. They become slaves to the telephone—resulting, of course, in pressure and stress. The only alternative is to take steps to control the phone. Otherwise, it may well control you.

There are people who control their telephone by taking the receiver off the hook. In this way, they aren't bothered during times when, for various valid reasons, they need a respite from the telephone's persistent ring. The individual who attempts to call in and disrupt their peace and quiet gets a perpetual busy signal. Once I happened to mention this technique in a meeting and received an immediate reaction from a woman in the audience who informed me that she worked for the telephone company. She was upset because she felt that it was the wrong thing to do. Nevertheless, it does work, and more than one person has learned to protect himself from the insistence of the phone in this way.

Popular today is an electronic "answering service" which plays a prerecorded sound track of the owner's voice, and then records the message and phone number of the caller. In this way, the call can be returned at the owner's convenience. Such devices are not only used by people who are absent from their offices or homes, but also by those who are there, but need to be free from the disturbance of the telephone at certain times.

Many well-organized businesses have developed a policy that limits incoming phone calls to certain hours of the day. For example, secretaries may be instructed to accept phone calls (unless otherwise specified) only between the morning hours of eleven and twelve o'clock. Or incoming calls may be limited to the hour between one and two in the afternoon—or to any other arbitrary time, for that matter. This enables a busy person to work uninterrupted during most of the day, and he can arrange his work so that calls during the specified hours do not bother him appreciably.

Then there are some people with the gift of gab. Whenever they call, they talk, and talk, and never seem to run down. Their talking is like a stream of conscious thought. Whatever pops into their minds turns into words and spills out to you over the phone. Even one such inconsiderate caller can slice a big hunk out of your valuable time and put you way off-schedule. Such thoughtlessness can cause you to feel frustrated and angry as you belabor the pressure of being behind in your work. Thus, tension builds up. The best way to handle such insensitive phone intruders is to be honest and frank with them. Thank them for calling, but let them know that you only have a limited time to converse. If necessary, give them a time limit—perhaps five minutes—and tell them that it is all the time you have right now. When the time is up, you probably will need to cut into the conversation and politely explain that you have "obligations" which make it necessary for you to say "good-bye." Then say it, and hang up. If you can't do this, then you've got a hang-up yourself.

The Unexpected

There's nothing to mess up your plans like the unexpected. Just when you think things are running smoothly, along comes the unanticipated to throw a monkey wrench in the routine. These "upsets" can be threatening and stressful unless you learn how to deal with them.

It has been said that we should expect the unexpected. Although this seems like a paradox, there is truth in it. In other words, don't pinch your schedule so tight—give yourself room to stretch. In this way you'll have a little leeway when the unexpected pops up and you'll be able to roll with the punches.

Another way to expect the unexpected is to be ready for it. This means advanced preparation. The student who keeps up with his studies doesn't fall apart when the teacher springs a pop quiz. And if you're the family chef, try doubling the amount that you would normally prepare and let your freezer keep that casserole or cake for the "surprise" dinner guest.

Sometimes, its even possible to sidestep the unexpected. By avoiding traps and pitfalls you are often able to avert a problem or a delay. For example, by keeping your roof in good repair, you are prepared when rainstorms come. Your neighbor, on the other hand, who is not as conscientious about home repairs, is struggling with an "unexpected" leak in his living room. The water dripping through has not only caused a big yellowish ring on the white ceiling but has stained a comparatively new divan.

No one ever *expects* to run out of gas; yet people do it all the time. To avoid this embarrassment and inconvenience, the driver must keep a check on the fuel indicator and not allow it to get too low. Even in periods of fuel shortage, a little preplanning is all it takes to keep rolling. To watch a fuel gauge is a lot less frustrating and a lot less time consuming than it is to run out of gas.

The Sublime to the Ridiculous

Distractions come in a myriad of forms and sizes, ranging from the sublime to the ridiculous. Sometimes, like a fly buzzing 'round your head, distractions can be just plain aggravating. Even a little thing like a hum in the light fixture can annoy you when you're trying to think. A barking dog, boisterous children, a temperamental typewriter, and a thousand other seemingly trivial disturbances can bother you enough to reduce your efficiency.

Pleasurable experiences can also detract from the business at hand. For example, our son, Kevin, is musical and especially enjoys the classics. When he was in the ninth grade he mentioned the fact that one of his high school teachers played classical recordings as a background when giving exams.

"It's beautiful and I love it," Kevin told us, "but I wish the teacher wouldn't do that. I find it awfully hard to concentrate on what I'm writing because my mind keeps wanting to follow the music."

Yes, the lovely and the pleasant can distract. In a sense, it charms you away from something less inviting. Even a warm spring day can allure your thoughts from their power of concentration and slow down your productivity.

According to Greek mythology, seamen of old faced a serious version of this problem. The legendary Sirens (sea nymphs who lived on an island in the sea) sang so beautifully that their music was irresistible; thus they lured passing sailors to the island's rocky shores—and to their death. Homer's *Odyssey* tells how Ulysses safeguarded himself and his crew from the sweet music of the Sirens by putting wax in his sailors' ears, and having his crew tie him to the mast. In this way, the sailors could not hear the Siren's singing, and Ulysses (although he heard their song) did not go to them.

Although it is unlikely that you will ever resort to being tied to a mast, there are times when you must take steps to protect yourself from seemingly pleasant distractions that could get you off-course and destroy you. It's hard to resist the pull of pleasure, especially when the other side of the balance spells duty. But, sometimes it is necessary, and in the long haul, it's worth it.

Physical problems can also interfere. It's hard to keep your mind on something when you are suffering. A nagging back pain, a headache, a toothache, the sniffles, a sore toe, or just plain fatigue can disrupt both your mental and physical processes. Unfortunately, the distraction will continue as long as the ailment persists. The solution comes only as the problem is relieved.

Worry or concern—or any emotional upset, for that matter—can also distract your mind and prevent you from putting out your best. It's a known fact that emotional turmoil is one of the primary causes of accidents in our mechanized society. Furthermore, emotional distractions are extremely difficult to control in that the source is internal rather than external. If the emotional distraction is more than a small, temporary upset, it is best to seek counsel from a qualified therapist.

Keeping on the Main Track

Even in the most ideal circumstances, there are bound to be at least a few distractions. They are here to stay and life will never be free from them.

The important issue, however, is not whether there are or are not distractions, but how you react toward them. You can let interruptions get the best of you—or you can make the best of them. You can go to pieces over a disrupted schedule, or you can put it together again and go on from there. You can either let distractions get you down, or you can come out on top. In other words, you can become all the stronger because you have learned to cope with them. It's up to you.

Some of man's greatest accomplishments have been produced under the most adverse surroundings. When the famous French physicists, Marie and Pierre Curie, made their great Nobel prize-winning discovery of radium, it was in a dilapidated old shed. It had a dirt floor and a skylight roof which leaked when it rained. In winter, it was freezing: in summer, the heat was stifling. To make matters worse, there was no chimney to carry off noxious gases. It was hardly the modern, well-equipped laboratory you'd expect for such a tremendous scientific breakthrough.

Albert Schweitzer, that brilliant German medical missionary, used a chicken coop for his first consultation room in the jungles of Africa. Through cracks in the slats of the lean-to, curious natives often peered and jabbered in a strange tongue. Distracting? Most definitely. But that didn't stop Albert Schweitzer. Over the years he built a large hospital and medical station where thousands of Africans were treated each year.

Distractions don't need to deter. If you really are serious about doing your job and doing it well, it's possible to become so engrossed in your work that you are not even aware of many would-be distractions. Serious students, for example, can learn to cut out extraneous influences and concentrate on the subject matter they are attempting to master. It can be done, and many have done it.

Most distractions are superficial. If these top-layer distractions bother you, then you are only working on a top-layer, superficial level of concentration. You need to dig a little deeper and plant your concentration there.

Are you concentrating on distractions or on the job? When you're aware of every little disturbance, your mind can't possibly be intent upon your work. All too often your concern over the distraction is an indication of a lack of interest. It doesn't take much to get you off the track because you aren't really enjoying the "ride."

Satan will sidetrack you if he can. If he can trick you into thinking that a distraction is really your primary function, he will have led you on a detour far from God's main track for your life. Or he may get you involved with so many secondary influences (all kinds of distractions) that you don't have time to do God's will. You may still say that God is your first priority, but in actuality, He isn't. And if Satan can't get you in either of those ways he'll try to cause you to become uptight and disagreeable about the interruptions and the people who cause them. Then to top it off, he'll weigh you down with a load of pressure because you're behind in your work.

Satan worked overtime in his attempt to distract the Apostle Paul from his steadfastness of purpose "to testify the gospel of the grace of God." Paul's distractions weren't little interruptions like most of us experience: they were big disruptions. . .like being thrown into prison, being shipwrecked, and almost being stoned to death. But in spite of these and many other disturbing elements, Paul kept on the "main track" and remained firm in his purpose.

". . .But none of these things shall move me. . .so that I might finish my course with joy" (the testimony of Paul, Acts 20:24).

7. Planned or Pressured

We hear a lot today about being *organized*. It's this quality of organization that not only helps get the job done, but helps get it done fast and well. When you are organized, you save yourself time, embarrassment, and much needless pressure. If for no other reason, learning to organize is worth it just from the standpoint of reducing tension and stress.

According to Webster, you are organized if you arrange your activities and your way of life in a systematic, orderly fashion. In other words, you understand your goals and you plan ahead to achieve them.

Lots of people would like to be organized, but they don't know how. They admire others who seem to have the "gift" of organization, but they *excuse* themselves on the basis of not having been born with this ability. Then they let it go at that.

Actually, anyone can *learn* to be organized. It's true that some seem to be endowed with orderly minds and natural aptitudes for logic, while others appear to be totally lacking along such lines. Nevertheless, a person's ability to organize is influenced by his experiences and can be developed or improved.

There are several important directives in learning to organize. A weakness in any area can disrupt the process.

Let's take a look at the basic framework for organization. If you can identify a weakness, you have probably spotted a point of pressure.

62
HOW TO HANDLE PRESSURE

Know Where You're Going

I once heard of a young man who was walking along a road when he met some acquaintances. After a mutual greeting, they inquired as to where he was going.

"I don't know," the young man replied, "I'll have to find out when I get there."

Multitudes go through life in just such confusion. They wander about with no goal or direction, trying this and that, not knowing what they want nor what it is they are seeking. It is sheer frustration to live such an empty, aimless existence.

This state of affairs is nothing new. Down through the centuries of time, the human race has been searching for something it hasn't found. When Jesus walked upon this earth, his heart was saddened because he saw that this was the condition of the people to which he had come. "And seeing the multitudes, He (Jesus) felt compassion for them, because they were distressed and downcast like sheep without a shepherd" (Matthew 9:36).

It would have been impossible for Jesus to have felt compassion without providing a remedy for the problems of these people He loved. Since they were "like sheep without a shepherd," Christ resolves their dilemma by revealing Himself as the solution. "I am the good shepherd," He said. "The good shepherd lays down His life for His sheep" (John 10:11).

Christ is indeed "the good shepherd." Not only did He lay down His life for the sheep, but He took it up again (John 10:17, 18). He lives today as the Good and Eternal Shepherd for all who follow Him.

When we allow Jesus to be our Good Shepherd, He clarifies our goals and gives our lives direction. He also adds the richness of a new dimension and states it as a purpose of His coming: "I came that they might have life, and that they might have it abundantly" (John 10:10). Without a doubt, this is the secret of a full and meaningful life.

Since God is our Shepherd of Love and provides us with "abundant life," we know that He cares and is personally interested in everything that pertains to us. He has given us His Word as an infallible guidebook for living. In addition, we have open access to Him through prayer, and can talk with Him at any time, anywhere, about anything. This includes our plans, our activities, and our goals.

Yes, purpose and motivation are included in the blessings of our Christian walk. Direction is no longer a problem, because God leads the way. But there are still responsibilities along the way. We still face the challenges of daily living, and often this is where the going gets rough.

It's rough many times, because we're too shortsighted. We fail to look ahead and see the rocks that lie across our pathway. Naturally, if we saw them and knew they were there, we'd move the rocks, or step around them—but we wouldn't fall over them.

That's the way it is in many of our daily activities. We must look ahead and make preparations in advance. In this way, we can avoid needless stress. It's wrong to blame God for pressures that we bring upon ourselves by our poor planning and negligence.

Nearly every activity of life requires at least some measure of direction. Whether cooking, gardening, going into business, teaching a class, directing a choir, or anything else, we do the job better when we have a basic plan in mind. God wants our lives to be efficient. "He is not the author of confusion" (1 Corinthians 14:33, 40) and it is not pleasing to God when His children live in confusion and disorder.

Policies and Procedures

It may be possible (although not recommended) that one person alone could go through life "playing it by ear." But when two, or more must work together it's a different story.

For example, when a dreamy-eyed young couple seal their troth with solemn "I do's," from that moment on their status changes. No longer are they two individual solos. They are now a duet, two working as one. As such, they will now need to establish guidelines and policies for their own home.

When children enter the family circle, policies in behavioral expectations become increasingly essential. A son, a daughter, each member of the family needs to know what does and what doesn't go. In a sense, the family is a little corporation—a unit consisting of a given number of members. In order for the family corporation to function efficiently and smoothly, there must of necessity be a set of rules—understood by all, and enforced. This means that each family member must know what is expected of him and what the consequences will be if he doesn't fulfill the requirements.

Some families find it helpful to spell it out with paper and pen. Others have a verbal understanding. The method is not important as long as it meets the needs of the family.

In other organizations there are no options. Whether it be insurance adjusters, a nursery school, a construction company, a church, or the local school board—in order to function properly they must have written policies and procedures. This eliminates the problem of guesswork. It's most disconcerting to wander around in uncertainty, wondering if you are fulfilling the requirements of the job. Unless there are guidelines that can be clearly defined in print, nearly everything that comes up is momentous and fraught with tension. But with a policy handbook or some other record of authorized procedures, problems can be solved before they develop, thus avoiding needless pressure.

Without written policies, an organization can expect to be under fire. There are bound to be serious conflicts and disagreements among personnel, creating a mountain of tension and stress. To keep such at a minimum, every member of an organization in every level of responsibility needs to know the goals and aspirations of the company, its policies and procedures and where his contribution fits into the scene.

Suggested methods and guidelines for doing a job can eliminate a great deal of confusion and misunderstanding. This is especially important for the orientation of new members in an organization. When goals and methods are clarified, a person is not plagued with bewilderment and a long process of trial and error. Much of the guesswork is removed and pressure is reduced for all concerned.

Plan and Prepare

Through the years, the *International Society of Boy Scouts* has maintained the wise and laudable motto, "Be prepared!" But it isn't necessary to be a boy scout to attest the prudence of this principle.

Preparedness is a good idea for anyone. As your competence grows, so does your confidence. The simple facts are that when you are prepared, you can handle a job with ease and efficiency. Even emergencies can be met as a challenge. It's a proven fact that when you are ready for tomorrow, its demands are not likely to become a source of pressure.

But being prepared for another day means planning and working today. Things don't just happen. You have to *make* them happen—and often it takes time.

This is a basic principle and applies to the momentous as well as the mundane. In fact, mundane matters probably suffer more from lack of planning than those which enjoy more prestige. Something momentous usually carries a measure of its own importance, whereas the mundane does not rate such distinction. But as for the mundane, there is much more of it, and, like the proverbial poor, it is "always with you." Thus, by virtue of its very common quality, it is often the object of oversight and neglect.

The consequences which result from lack of planning may run the gamut from the embarrassing, the hectic, to the disastrous. In most mundane situations, the results may not be necessarily embarrassing or disastrous, but they can be hectic.

There are many disorganized people who fall into the pattern of a hectic routine. It's most obvious, I suppose, in a home situation. For example, many households are a nightmare in the morning. Let's peek in on the Smith family.

It's a typical weekday morning in which the three Smith children and their father must meet the arrival-time deadlines of school and the office, respectively. The mother, (who, incidentally, overslept) is valiantly doing her utmost to activate her zapped-out children and yawning husband. She prods, pushes, preaches, helps, hounds, and hollers. The routine is exhausting for mom and unpleasant for everyone.

The clock ticks on and at last all beds are cleared of their occupants. There now begins a series of morning emergencies.

"Hey, Mom, make Tammy get out of the bathroom! She's in there trying to make herself gorgeous again. Mom, tell her to get out! She hogs the john every morning."

(Tammy is fourteen, and Bud, her brother and accuser, is eleven.)

After numerous shouts of disapproval intermingled with loud poundings on the bathroom door, Tammy screams back. "Leave me alone. I'm not comin' out yet. Go use the bathroom downstairs."

"I can't, Stupid. My toothbrush is up here."

Another cry of distress resounds from another room. This time it is seven-year-old Debbie.

"Mommie, Mommie. I can't find my other shoe. Have you seen my shoe?"

After a desperate search in cluttered closets and under beds, mom manages to turn up a small green sneaker under the dining room table.

"Honey," hubby yells from the bedroom, "where's my blue striped shirt?"

Oh, dear, mom remembers, it was in the laundry yesterday. It's washed but not ironed. But hubby has a special luncheon today and needs that particular shirt. So mom heats up the iron and gives the striped shirt a quickie. It's not too good but it will have to do.

Mom is rushing around trying to throw some peanut butter sandwiches together for the kids' lunches when Tammy walks into the kitchen. Now it's mom's turn to complain.

"You're not wearing that weird outfit, are you? It looks awful. Go change it." This was the beginning of a short but furious battle in which neither side won.

Breakfast is not much of an issue. It's sort of a touch and go affair. Mom used to fix bacon and eggs or hot cereal once in a while, but there was always so much confusion, and half the time everyone was in too much of a hurry to eat, so she got discouraged and quit. Now it's usually Post Toasties or Raisin Bran, with everyone on his own.

Bud and his father are both seated at the kitchen table, gulping down their respective cold cereals. In between mouthfuls, Bud scribbles out a last minute English assignment and keeps trying to extract answers from dad who is scanning the morning paper. Glancing at his watch, Mr. Smith stands up and announces he must leave.

But dear me, where are his glasses! He has to have his glasses. He's not licensed to drive without them.

So mom and Bud both join the search for the missing glasses, but it is Debbie who finally spots them on the piano bench.

And so it goes. . .until the last young Smith is shoved out the door and exhorted to hurry so she won't be late.

Whew! The "tornado" has abated and mom finds herself standing in the midst of the debris. She sighs, pours herself a cup of coffee and flops down in an easy chair to recuperate from the ordeal she has just been through.

"I think I'm allergic to morning," she groans.

And well she might be. Mornings are habitually turbulent. This day is no exception. In fact, many times it's worse.

Only yesterday the process of dressing reduced second-grade Debbie to tears because she couldn't find any underwear. You see, she's going through a "stage" right now where she changes her clothes—all of them—several times a day. It caught up with her yesterday morning. All her undies were in the hamper.

And it seems as though someone is always losing something. Books, notebooks, assignments, PE clothes, permission slips all seem to have an uncanny sense for getting mislaid. Sometimes, by tearing the house upside down, the lost is finally found. Other times, things don't turn up until too late.

No, indeed, mornings are far from pleasant in the Smith household. Tempers soar, and clashes are inevitable. There is tension and stress . . .and intense pressure. It's a terrible way to start the day.

It doesn't need to be like that, however. The major problem is that the Smiths do not plan ahead. They leave everything to the last minute, and then find themselves in a bind with no way out.

Across the street live the Johnsons. Like the Smith family, they also have several school-age children. But it's a different story in the Johnson household.

They are quiet people and unassuming, but they are well-organized. From the time the children were small they were taught, by word and example, "a place for everything and everything in its place." In this way, they never have the problem of finding things when they want them. It's an old fashioned cliche—but it works.

The Johnsons are also great believers in planning their work ahead and doing it early. "Work before play," the children are taught. Another cliche—but working well! The children have grown up accepting the fact that you don't consider something like TV unless you have your work done *first*.

Before the Johnson children go to bed, they choose and lay out their clothing for the next day. (This eliminates the pressure building possibilities of finding only one shoe, or having no underwear.) They also gather their books and assignments and have them ready for the morning. Because they are so well-organized, the children are able to make their own beds and tidy their rooms before leaving for school, (something that the Smith youngsters seldom find time to do).

Planning ahead is a way of life for the Johnsons. Lunches are made the night before and kept in the refrigerator until morning. Before retiring, Mrs. Johnson sets the table in preparation for breakfast. In this way the family can sit down together in the morning and enjoy a nourishing breakfast. After breakfast, they read a short passage of Scripture before the children go to school and Mr. Johnson leaves for work.

If the Johnsons seem unreal to you, you may be admitting that you are disorganized. Perhaps you are weak in the area of planning. Many people are. Although the roots of disorganization often stem from the home, its undesirable influence follows a person into every aspect of life. Don, for example, consistently gets himself in a jam. He's a salesman, an eight-cylinder one, but only functioning on two. He leaves everything until the last minute, then becomes frustrated. For Don, and for most people, learning to organize by planning ahead would solve a great many problems.

Students are notorious for putting off term papers and other long-range assignments until the eleventh hour. Although they may have had weeks in which to prepare a report, they don't do much about it until a few days before it's due. The result, of course, is pressure—plenty of it.

Exams reveal the same weakness. Although students are well aware that tests and exams are inevitable, all too often they postpone studying until the last minute and then attempt to cram. Trying to assimilate enormous amounts of information in one sitting, or staying up the entire night before an exam, are poor substitutes for a consistent daily pattern of study. The pressure on students who do not know how to plan ahead and organize their time is tremendous. The majority of college and university dropouts are victims of this problem. It's enough to give anyone a breakdown.

68
HOW TO HANDLE PRESSURE

The Indispensable List

Planning ahead and wisely budgeting your time is one of the best favors you can do for yourself. One way to accomplish this is through the use of a list. Meals, shopping, entertaining, public speaking, school assignments, and traveling are just a few of the areas in which a list is an indispensable aid. When you list the jobs to be done and plan it out on paper, it helps to clarify and organize your work. You are more efficient because you don't waste time and energy by backtracking, neither do you forget to care for important details. Best of all, it keeps pressure from sapping your energies and makes the job at hand a challenge rather than a chore.

When packing for a trip, for example, you don't have to rush around the last minute trying to decide what to take with you. You can plan in advance by writing that handy little list. Begin with the various categories that should be included in your packing, and leave room under each for a more detailed notation of your needs. Naturally, a major category is clothing. List all the clothes you might need. A few days before you are scheduled to leave, see to it that the clothes you want are ready to go. This eliminates the rush and pressure of last minute washing, ironing, mending, sewing and other such preparations.

Another category is medication. It's extremely disconcerting to develop an itch and not have anything available to abate it. And it's rough to sneeze and sniffle with hayfever with nothing to relieve you of your misery. Even a good dose of vacation sunburn is hard to take with nothing to help soothe your crimson, blistered skin. And of course, you don't want to forget your toothbrush. It's a small item—but large in importance.

Most important of all is your Bible. If you must forget something, let it be something else, but not the Word of God. You may also want a camera, and film, and stationery supplies.

If your travel is taking you to foreign lands, there'll be certain needs (other than passports) for which you must prepare, like a transformer for your electrical gadgets that will let you use the higher voltage and direct current of those countries. If you use an electric shaver and forget this little item, you may find yourself growing a beard.

And so the list goes on—thought through and written down in a logical order so it can be checked and double-checked. It's a simple thing, but amazingly helpful. It relieves the pressures of packing and the pressures of not having what you need when you arrive at your destination. Furthermore, it's not always convenient (or even possible) to buy what you need if your travels take you to places like Podunk or Patagonia.

Incidentally, once you have made what you consider a comprehensive list, save it and use it again for other vacations or trips. It's a great time-saver and relieves much of the pressure of packing. We're called upon to do a great deal of traveling, and this is the way we prepare.

Trying to trust too much to your memory can be a point of pressure. Sometimes your mind gets cluttered with too many details: it's hard to sort them out and find the right thoughts at the right times. In other words, you temporarily forget. But when you write things on a list it helps to organize ideas in your mind as well as give you something tangible to use for reference. The fact is, you'll usually remember a thing a lot better after you've had the kinesthetic experience of writing it.

The Wise and the Foolish

The busier you are, the more you need to plan ahead and prepare. A busy woman I know is often called upon to entertain large groups. Sometimes there are fifty, seventy-five, ninety or even a hundred or more people who come for dinner. People who know her, and realize that her schedule is a busy one even without entertaining these groups, often ask her how she keeps everything going so smoothly.

"I plan it all out several days in advance," she explains. "I write everything down that needs to be done, and then plan what must be accomplished each day. Then every day I check my list and make sure I do the things that are scheduled for that day. I plan it so that I have most of the work done ahead of time. Then when my guests arrive I am more relaxed and can be a better hostess."

"Besides," she added, "there always seems to be plenty to do the last minute anyhow. I'm not pressured when I plan my work ahead, but I sure would be if I didn't."

I couldn't help but contrast this gracious well-organized hostess with a scatterbrained woman I knew some years ago. She and her family had moved from the city to a rural area in another part of the state. At that time I was traveling with a gospel team, and when my friend discovered that we were scheduled to be at a church in her area on a certain Sunday, she phoned and insisted that we all come to her home for dinner after the morning service. I warned her that there would be five of us, but she said that would be fine.

I'll never forget that Sunday. She met us at church and after the service, gave us directions for finding the house. But when we got there and walked through the door, we were due for a shock. "Had we made a mistake?" we all wondered.

70
HOW TO HANDLE PRESSURE

From all appearances, one would never suspect that she was expecting company. The house was in a total uproar. Seldom have I seen a place in such a mess, especially when guests were coming. What's more, no preparations had been made for a meal. Yet, our friend had definitely invited us—yes, insisted that we come for dinner. And here we were. I wondered what would happen.

As it turned out, there was only one thing to do. We all pitched in and worked. Some of us peeled potatoes and fried the chicken while others washed a stack of leftover dirty dishes and pots and pans. Then we cleared the clutter from the dining room table and chairs so we would have a place to put the food and something on which to sit.

When at last we sat down to eat, our poor hostess was in a daze. I don't believe she had ever experienced such a flurry of activity as that which took place in her home that afternoon. In apparent embarrassment and chagrin, she thanked us for our help and confessed that she had never learned to organize. Although this was quite obvious, we were courteous and told her we appreciated her kindness.

After dinner, our gang pitched in and cleaned up the dishes. Some of us even "walked the extra mile" by doing other household chores such as making the beds. Later in the afternoon, as we drove away from that home, we knew one thing; we had left it much better than we had found it.

Although we laughed about the whole ridiculous episode, our hearts went out in pity to our disorganized but well-meaning hostess.

Although it's imprudent not to prepare for guests when you have invited them, it is equally as foolish not to make preparations for many other occasions. When you know that Christmas is coming (you've had a whole year's notice), why wait until December 24th to do your shopping?

Perhaps you've heard about the ten young ladies who were on their way to a wedding. Five of the girls were wise and had prepared for the trip, making certain that they had sufficient fuel. But the other five didn't give it a thought. Although they had started out in the afternoon while it was still light, they had a long way to go. In time it became dark. It was then that the five foolish virgins realized that they had no oil in their lamps.

Jesus tells that the poor, foolish girls had no recourse but to turn around and try to find a place where they could buy some oil. But in going back, they lost a great deal of time and were unable to return in time for the wedding (Matthew 25:1-13).

To plan ahead and be prepared is helpful in many areas of life, but in nothing is it more important than in preparing for eternity.

The Thief

There's an old axiom which points the accusing finger at procrastination as the culprit who has shortchanged us on time.

Time is a precious commodity. We only have it once, and then it's gone—forever. To waste time, or to "kill" it is wrong. The Bible admonishes us to *redeem* time. (See Colossians 4:5 and Ephesians 5:16.) If you have time on your hands, you'd better busy them and accomplish something.

The purpose of planning and scheduling is to help you get the job done. But all the planning in the world is useless unless you make the effort to follow through. What good is a time schedule if you close your eyes and ignore it?

Putting off a job that you know should be done ranks high among the causes of pressure. First, there's the pressure of guilt because you know you've been delinquent about doing your duty. Before you know it, the "tomorrow" when you were going to do it is here—and you must offer more excuses to postpone doing the job a little longer. (More guilt—but not enough to bring about a change.)

Jobs don't get done unless somebody does them. If you have a responsibility, you're the one to see that it gets done. To delay a duty doesn't make it any easier. The pressure, however, of work undone continues to hang heavy over your head. The longer you wait, the heavier it becomes. It's like living under a weight.

"If I wait long enough, maybe I won't have to do it." Some people seem to hold this feeble philosophy. It's true that if you wait long enough, someone might come along and do it for you. (This adds more pressure because he dislikes you for being so lazy.) It's also true that when you delay you often miss out on an opportunity to achieve or to progress. (More guilt and more pressure.)

Most of the time, however, a job waits to be done. Then suddenly, the deadline looms before you. It's the eleventh hour and you have much to do. The hurry, flurry, rush and push that come as a result of your procrastination take their toll in your emotional and physical well being. The pressure is tremendous.

It doesn't need to be this way. Budget your time, then make an effort to keep within your budget. The relief you'll feel from knowing that the job is completed will more than compensate for the effort.

So keep in mind that "one of these days" is "none of these days." And procrastination is *truly* the thief of time.

Not Too Tight

Remember when you were a youngster and your folks bought you a new pair of shoes? The salesman would slip the shoe on your foot and then feel the end of it to be sure your toes had some room left for growing. The shoes had to fit correctly. They had to be the right length, the right width, the right heel size—just suited to your personal needs. Your parents knew that ill-fitting shoes would be harmful to your feet.

So they chose shoes for you that were not too large: such would be awkward and clumsy. Not too small: they would hurt because they would cramp your feet. The perfect fit for your new shoes, you discovered, gave your toes plenty of room to wiggle without losing your foot in the shoe.

Planning a schedule for yourself follows much the same principle. Like a shoe, your plan is a supportive measure that sets limits and protects you from outside influences. But it must be suited to you and your individual needs. If it isn't, it won't work.

It's important that your activities are compatible with the time you have allotted them. In other words, be realistic about your schedule and don't pack it too full. When you plan too large a job or too many assignments for an insufficient amount of time, you do not reduce pressure: you add to it. So judge your job and match it carefully with the right amount of time. Too tight a schedule cramps your ability and prevents you from doing your best. Furthermore, it discourages you from sticking with it. Using again the analogy of the shoe; when it's too tight, you won't wear it. When your routine squeezes too hard, it's only natural that you'll discard it.

Not only should your schedule be comfortable, it should give you some "room for growing." A little leeway can be a lifesaver at times when things take longer than you think they will. Besides there are always those little extras that you don't anticipate.

Of course, too much of a "hang loose" schedule isn't practical either. That's an excellent way *not* to get things done. The fact is, you need to budget your time if you hope to get much accomplished. But it must be reasonable and workable, within your comfortable reach, or it won't do the job.

The Framework's Not of Steel

Most everything works better when it's planned. The haphazard and casual are great for relaxation, but usually, not for accomplishment. Unless, of course, the casual happens to be planned. Sometimes it takes a sizable amount of planning to make a project appear unplanned.

But there *is* a place for the *spontaneous*. Most definitely. Many of the greatest ideas of all time have been the products of spontaneity. The spontaneous is warm and expressive. It is the real person shining through. This is something that we can't afford to do without.

Spontaneity cannot flourish, however, inside a framework of steel. An atmosphere of rigidity and restrictiveness is lethal to its sensitive and fragile nature. In order for spontaneity to survive, there must be an emotional climate of acceptance and flexibility.

A first cousin to spontaneity, is another sparkling charmer—*creativity*! We laud the creative as an essence of greatness. But original thought, although not as emotionally delicate as spontaneity, must also be cultivated in fertile ground. Ideas precast in concrete do not make likely planting beds for seeds of originality.

Since creativity, by its very nature, must deviate from the status quo, it is obvious that this quality is incompatible with rigid, inflexible procedures. Innovative ideas need room to grow and develop. To confine them within the limits of a die-cast, forged iron framework is to doom them to their death. Originality is the product of freedom, not restrictiveness.

What, then, does this tell us about predetermined plans and preset procedures? Are not the concepts of spontaneity and creativity at odds with the principles of organization? At first glance, they appear to be standing on opposite sides of the fence, fiercely hurling contradictions at one another. In reality, they *need* one another.

When God created our world—He made *everything* in perfect balance. This applies to all aspects and every detail of life. The system of checks and balances did not originate with the founding fathers of our democratic republic. It was God's idea. Eons before man existed, God proved the importance of balance as he flung the universe into space and spun our little planet in its ecliptical solar orbit. God's system of balance keeps the world and all that is in it running smoothly and efficiently. Only when things become lopsided or off-center, do they lose their efficiency and create a problem.

Yes—there has to be a balance. The planned and the organized. The spontaneous and the creative. Both are important, and both are needed.

Although it's essential to organize your time and schedule your activities, remember that you are building a framework—not a fortress. The purpose of planning is to improve development, not impede it. When plans are made to serve the people, they are successful: but when people are hampered by their own restrictive arrangements, planning becomes a travesty.

74
HOW TO HANDLE PRESSURE

A rigid, inflexible schedule seldom meets the needs of every individual. How can it when all of us are different with different potential and different needs? What's more, we ourselves are in a constant state of flux. What met our needs yesterday is inadequate for today. Although some conform more easily than others, there are always a few free thinkers and rugged individualists who find it difficult to fit into a precut mold. When they are forced into a routine that is brittle and unbending, something is likely to give. When this happens, unfortunately the entire structure is often discarded, whereas the real problem is not the structure but its inflexibility.

Yet, creativity can benefit from a certain amount of supportive structure. Like a rose clinging to a trellis, it needs the help and reinforcement of a structured situation in order to encourage growth in a meaningful direction. Few great artists or musicians or writers produced their masterpieces simply for the love of it. Oh, I'm sure they loved their work, but that's just the point. It *was* their work. They were commissioned to do specific paintings or sculptures, or they were asked to compose special music for certain occasions. These were paid jobs. Although they utilized their creative talents, the projects were structured for them along certain limits.

Planning is meant to lend you support, not to crush you beneath its weight. When the plans that were meant to ease your pressure become pressure in themselves, remember that you're still in charge. A schedule is made to serve you: you are *not* its slave.

8. People Problems

There's nothing in this world that has as much influence on people as other people. People bring each other joy, as well as heartache. They help, and they hinder. They have the capacity to encourage, or discourage; they can build, or they can destroy.

The interactions among people are both varied and complicated. Most of all, they are needed.

Long before a baby's mind begins to shape tangible memories, his relationships with people are molding his personality. As he grows and matures, his associations with others will widen and deepen. All through his life, people will continue to be the pivotal factors of his emotions. Because of people, his life will be sprinkled with laughter and will have its share of tears. And because of people, he will know tension, and worry, and pressure.

If people weren't so important to one another, they would not affect each other so deeply. But they are immensely important, and human relationships reach into every area of life. It's little wonder, then, that people are affected by misunderstandings, concerns, and many other people problems. (See Romans 14:7.)

You Can't Leave Home

The closest unit in human experience is the family. It stands to reason then, that family members influence one another in countless ways. Your habits, your thinking, your health, and most of all, your emotions are all affected by the relationships you share with the rest of your family.

When things aren't going well at home, you can be sure that the stress you feel will also show itself in other ways. You may be accident-prone, or overly sensitive to criticism. You may find it hard to keep your mind on your work; you may make foolish mistakes; or you may get behind in your work. Some people become nervous and upset; still others become defensive and argumentative. There's nothing like home pressures to bring out your hostility.

Teachers know that problem children are often expressing the insecurities of a poor home situation. A divorce, for example, is trauma for a child. It's a pressure which he is unable to justify or resolve. In the classroom, it may show itself in failing grades, aggressive behavior, or even in becoming sullen and withdrawn.

Suicides, crime, and a host of other social offenses can be traced to unhealthy relationships in the home. Of course, the majority will never be the victims of such radical reactions. Let's hope not. Nevertheless, everyone reacts in one way or another to unpleasant family stimuli and home pressures. You are no exception.

You may be upset about many things. Perhaps you're worried about a loved one who is seriously ill or must undergo a major operation. Your emotional involvement will not allow you to shove the anxiety from your mind. Furthermore, such concerns and worries are not limited to your immediate family: married sons and daughters, in-laws, grandchildren, grandparents, aunts, uncles and anyone close to you can be an object of your anxiety.

You may be concerned about an abnormal child. Will he be able to find a place for himself in life? Or you may be upset because of arguments and disagreements among members of the family. Your teen-age son or daughter may be in a state of rebellion, and you're at wit's end to know what to do.

It might be that your husband is an alcoholic. Or maybe it's your mother-in-law who's giving you a bad time; or your daughter-in-law may be continuously cutting you down.

Perhaps you're worried and upset because you and your spouse have not been getting along. You want to make a go of it, but you have reason to believe that he or she has been unfaithful. Your marriage is tottering, and you know it.

These, and many other life concerns, are sources of enormous pressure. When you are weighed down with domestic worries, you cannot shed them, even though you may want to. You can try to bury them under a whole new set of interests, but they are there, nevertheless still seething and boiling underneath. But they are destined to surface again.

77
PEOPLE PROBLEMS

Many of the pressures you feel today are remnants of childhood tensions and misunderstandings. Your attitudes, your hang-ups, your way of life, most of what you are today resulted from experiences and relationships that took place in those impressionable years of your youth. In a sense, your childhood will always be with you.

So, like it or not, you are never truly free from the stresses and concerns which dominate you in the context of your home. Family pressures follow you into every situation of life. Whether in school, at work, or downtown doing your shopping, the problems of home and family, either consciously or unconsciously, influence your thinking, your choices, your behavior and your pressures throughout the day.

A Friend Indeed

Next to your family—and many times surpassing them—your strongest sphere of influence is your friends.

But friends, unlike family members, can be gained or lost. Perhaps it's this shaky association that causes many people to be kinder and more courteous to friends than they are to their families. You can't lose a mother or a brother—but you can lose a friend. The fact is that friendships, however warm and accepting, are never free from the potential of a broken relationship.

The status of a person's friendship varies with circumstances, time and location. The private who might have been your best buddy when you were doing your stint overseas soon becomes a memory when you're back in civilian life. When that childhood chum with whom you shared everything (lunches, homework, secrets and colds) was uprooted from your neighborhood by parents who moved to another state, you were lonesome for a little while, but in time you substituted another "best friend."

For some, the insecurity of a friend relationship can be an area of enormous pressure. Misunderstandings or disagreements become extremely threatening. In order not to lose rapport, many (especially young people) are willing to sacrifice their standards and ambitions to the dictates of their friends. This, of course, creates an even greater pressure, without, as they had hoped, strengthening the ties of their friendships.

Peer pressure is a compelling force among the young. There's no denying that. And many do not survive the pressure exerted upon them by their godless friends. But peer pressure need not produce peer problems. It only becomes a problem when a young person associates with the *wrong* peers. To assure the right peer relationships, keep your family actively involved in an ongoing, Christ-centered church. Choose one with a strong youth-emphasis and godly leadership. Christian schools are also important in nurturing desirable associations. Encourage friendships with dedicated Christians. This kind of peer relationship will help to establish a personal relationship with Jesus. There is no better safeguard against the peer pressure of the godless.

But youth is not alone in being influenced by friends. Everyone reacts to the opinions of others. You want your friends to admire you and to think well of you. So when friends are coming for dinner, of course you'll use your fancy china; and you'll find time to wash the car before taking friends for a drive. You adjust your activities, your dress and your conversation to the tastes and interests of your friends. Unconsciously, you may even monitor your lives by "What will the Joneses think?"

The desire to be accepted and admired by others creates a powerful point of pressure and can prevent you from being real. If you have a low self-image, you may not feel worthy of acceptance, not to mention, admiration. Yet, you want to be well thought of, and you need to feel a sense of belonging, so you develop an image, thinking that your friends won't know the difference between the real you and the person you want them to think you are. Unfortunately, this is a very shaky arrangement. The very people you want to impress can often see through the curtain, and they don't admire you for being phony.

There is one friend, however, who accepts you completely and unreservedly just as you are. He knows and understands the real you and that's the part He loves. He is a constant friend and companion who sticks closer than the closest of brothers. He is always with you wherever you go. He never changes, and His love and His loyalty can be trusted and relied upon "yesterday, today, and forever."

This wonderful friend is Jesus.

The Outside World

When you step outside of your circle of family and friends, your relationships are more shallow, and less emotional. You do not feel much deep concern for the needs of business associates, casual acquaintances and strangers because your interest in them is superficial or self-centered. When you go to the market, a few pleasantries may pass between you and the checkout clerk, but it's not a social visit and you both know it. If you talk very long, the supervisor will be quick to inform the employee that it had better not happen again.

Many of your nonemotional relationships involve business employees, employers, and associates. A person may be working for you as a plumber, a gardener, or a salesclerk, or you may be working for someone else. Even the self-employed have clientele to whom they have certain obligations to fulfill. Indeed, everyone is obligated to someone else, but it is definitely a business relationship. Courteous—but cold.

But business relationships are often far from courteous and many times they are not only cold—but frozen. With few exceptions, the business world is hard and calculating. Basically, it is interested in its own benefits.

Yet, as each individual goes about in his own self-centered way, he brings his personal pressures with him. When rubbing elbows with people of the outside world, we may inadvertently rub some of them the wrong way. Many people are deeply disturbed. Their maladjustments may not be sufficient to prevent them from functioning in a job. But it's enough to keep them on edge, ready to lock horns with anyone who gets in their way.

The Wrong Chemistry

"There's something about her that I just can't stand."

"I don't know exactly why, but he gets on my nerves."

"I know he's polite and all that, but he irks me."

Have you ever heard people make comments like these? I'm sure you have. And furthermore, although you may not be in the habit of passing judgment on others, you've probably felt that way about some people yourself.

Personality clashes are as old as the fall of man. From the time Adam accepted the forbidden fruit from Eve, and blamed her for their fallen predicament, people have been quick to jump to their self-defense. It doesn't take much to draw the battle lines.

Studies show that more people lose their jobs because of personality problems than for any other reason. These clashes can cause constant consternation.

Some people are hard to take. It doesn't pose much of a problem if the person that bothers you is someone whom you seldom see, or with whom you have little association. But when the person who turns you off is someone with whom you must work day after day, or relate to in any way other than a superficial manner, it can be hard to take. Conflicts and tensions are bound to arise from such a strained relationship. And when the offensive one happens to be your boss (or your spouse) you're in for big pressure trouble. To make matters worse, you either blame yourself for your bad attitude (which continues in spite of your blame) or you try to justify your feelings by convincing yourself that "X" is a villain.

This doesn't help much. In fact, it compounds your problem by causing you to feel guilty about something which you don't seem to be able to control.

The fact is, not all of us can expect to like everything about everyone else. I know that the Bible enjoins us to "love one another" (1 John 3:23). It is also true that Jesus places the commandment, "Thou shalt love thy neighbor as thyself" (Matthew 22:39) on a priority level second only to our love for God.

Love, yes. But it doesn't say anything about *like*.

The grim fact is that we don't even *like* everything about ourselves. And all too often, the very quality that we dislike in someone else, is one that we have ourselves. We dislike it in ourselves but we may be afraid to face up to it, so we rationalize or pretend it isn't there. But when someone else shows that same undesirable trait, all the hostility that has been repressed toward ourselves is directed at that unfortunate individual.

Sometimes we dislike a certain quality in another person because we sense a lack in ourselves. It's hard to measure your own weakness against another's strength. That's when the demon of jealousy moves in and whispers a green version of the sour grape theory into your eager ear. Your subconscious won't allow you to admit that what you feel is jealousy, and so you justify your attitude by being overly critical of the other person. You actually dislike that person because of this ability—and your own lack of it.

There are many reasons why you may feel a dislike for someone else. Some of them are based upon whims or impressions. These aren't too reliable. Other times, your cultures or your backgrounds are so divergent that you can't accept the differences. Besides that, people themselves are different. They have different temperaments, different interests and different levels of intelligence. After all, you can't expect everyone else to be as exciting as you are! To you, some may be plain boring—or even obnoxious. Their opinion of you may not be too complimentary either.

In a world so diverse as ours, there are bound to be characteristics about other people that you won't enjoy. How you react, however, is vital to your happiness and theirs.

First, realize that *everyone* who has ever walked this earth, with the exception of Christ, is a sinner and has faults. Indeed, human beings are far from perfect. As a member of the human race, you, too, have faults and weaknesses. Relatives and close friends are usually quick to verify this (grandparents excepted). Since you must recognize that you are not perfect, in all fairness, you must make the same allowances for someone else.

Second, realize that along with their faults, people *do* have some good points too. Sometimes you have to hunt to find them. Although their positive qualities may be well camouflaged, if you probe long enough and deep enough, you'll find your reward. Yes, all people have weaknesses, and all people have strengths. You must acknowledge this as a basic truth before you can make any progress.

Building upon this premise, the third point in your relationship with other people is to accept them for their strengths. Concentrate on their strong qualities, not their weaknesses. Sure they have faults, who doesn't? But if you focus on a person's good qualities instead of magnifying those which are less desirable, it will help your attitude immensely. You may even discover that you actually like that person. Oh, you still may not like some of the things he does, but you won't be bothered by those things as much when they are no longer the big issue.

The Unlovable

But what if after you've sincerely tried, you honestly can't find enough admirable qualities to hold your concentration? It's hard to focus on a strength, when it's so outnumbered by a person's weaknesses.

If this is the case, it's time to find the dynamics behind his distasteful behavior. The Narramore Christian Foundation has as its slogan "Every person is worth understanding." In your attempt to understand a person, keep in mind the basic psychological principle which states that all behavior is caused, and causes are always multiple. In other words, there are a number of reasons why a person acts the way he does. When you understand a person's background and realize what kind of experiences he has had to cause him to become the kind of person he is, you have an entirely different attitude. In other words, you've caught a glimpse of his handicaps. No longer do you feel condemnation, but rather pity and a desire to help.

The person may still be obnoxious, but you no longer feel threatened. You know now that it's his problem, not yours. He may still be disagreeable and hard to get along with, but it's easier to take when you realize that his hostility is not directed at you personally as much as it is an expression of his inner conflicts. You are the target of his anger only because you happen to be there.

But after all that, what if you still can't abide that person? He's hostile, he's surly, he's ungrateful and he's repulsive. In short, he's unlovable. He does nothing to deserve your love, so how does God expect you to love a wretched person like that?

In the first place, if he deserved your love, he wouldn't need it as much as he does by not deserving it. Furthermore, God doesn't withhold His love from the undeserving. If He did, we'd all be out on a limb, because no one, except Jesus, has ever deserved the love of God.

God specializes, however, in loving the unlovely. Sin is the most repulsive thing that God can ever encounter. He hates sin, "But God demonstrates His own love toward us, in that while we were yet sinners, Christ died for us" (Romans 5:8).

So when someone is undeserving, there isn't much about him that you can find to like, God can love that person through you. He can ease the pressure of dislike, and fill your heart with His love, even for the unlovable.

Improvers or Impeders

Dean had too much on the ball to be *stuck* in the warehouse all his life. The job there consisted of heavy work and unpredictable, undesirable hours. But Dean was healthy and strong, and the job paid fairly well. Its strange hours had actually been helpful to Dean while he was putting himself through college. Now, three years after his graduation, Dean was frustrated and bored with his job. The horrible thought that he might find himself working at the warehouse the rest of his life haunted him like a nightmare lurking in the corridors of his mind.

What Dean wanted to be was a psychologist. He loved people and enjoyed working with them (a far cry from being alone in the warehouse). But becoming a psychologist meant going back to school for several more years in order to get his doctor's degree. Dean was a good student, so that posed no problem. He was ready for a change and couldn't wait to get started.

The drawback was that two years ago he had gotten married. To get his doctorate would require nearly five more years of schooling. For Dean, it would be money going out with none coming in. For his wife it would mean that she would need to support them both. This idea did not appeal to her in the least. She had hoped to stay home and raise a family. Five years seemed a long time to wait. Besides, Dean's pay at the warehouse was not bad and they still needed so many things. No, she was not willing to sacrifice. She did not want her husband to go back to school.

And so Dean was held back from moving ahead. The very one who should have encouraged him to step out and develop his potential became a weight and a source of pressure.

All too often the people who ought to be backing you and lending you their support, are dragging their feet and holding you back. You'd like to move ahead, but they panic and gasp, "Not now." While they're waiting for the right moment, the opportunity slips by, and it's too late.

Or every time you come up with a progressive idea, they peer over their spectacles and mutter, "It can't be done."

Even small changes are met with resistance. "Oh, but it's never been done that way before," they inform you (as though you didn't know it). "We've always done it this other way and its been satisfactory enough. Let's not rock the boat."

And so you are stymied.

Some people seem to be inflicted with negativism. They look on the dark side of everything and their response to any request is invariably "no." It's difficult for a positive, forward looking person to continually throw off such a pile of wet blankets.

Many organizations run amuck because they are hampered by negative personnel. The people chosen for boards or committees are especially strategic. Whether it's the Ladies' Auxiliary or the Board of Directors, they can either be a source of help or a hindrance. They can produce pressure, or they can eliminate it.

One evening while dining at the home of a friend who was the head of an organization, my host graciously said to me, "The Board of Directors of our organization is meeting tonight. How'd you like to come with me and sit in on the meeting?"

I accepted his invitation, and the experience was a real eye-opener. After I was introduced I moved over to the side of the room and thumbed through the pages of a periodical while they transacted the business of their organization. I couldn't help but hear what was going on, however, and as the evening progressed, I noticed that one of the men challenged almost everything that was said. Another man seemed to oppose or criticize everything that was brought up. He wasn't happy, it seemed, unless he voted "against" the motion. Two others sat throughout the evening and scarcely said a word. If they had any opinions, they were left unexpressed. Still another character seemed to be a self-appointed jester. He busied himself thinking up clever statements and humorous little remarks. Most everything seemed funny to him, so he kept on cracking jokes.

After the meeting, when taking me back to my hotel, my friend remarked, "Well, that's the board I have to work with."

"Do they always function like that?" I asked.

My friend assured me that this meeting was typical. In other words, he was "stuck" with a number of board members who specialized in *impeding* rather than *improving*.

It's a source of real frustration and pressure when a leader (or anyone, for that matter) is forced to work with a board, or committee that doesn't function properly. I'm not suggesting for a moment that the members should be rubber stamps. "Yes men" defeat the intended purpose of any council or advisory body. But in order to be effective, the members must realize that they are individually responsible to carefully weigh and think through the needs of the organization which they serve. They should then seek to make a worthwhile contribution. In other words, they are the guardians of the organization: it is up to them to see that it succeeds.

There are committees, and there are committees. Some function smoothly and efficiently, but many do not. A board or a committee can be a blessing, or a serious burden. It can put itself up as a self-appointed tribunal and place other members of the organization under constant strain, or it can be a supportive unit that relieves the pressures of responsibility.

You may or may not be responsible for the people who comprise the boards and committees within your organization. But if this responsibility is in your hands, it's imperative that you select people carefully. Judge prospective members on the basis of: "What ability would he bring to the group?" "Is he basically a well-adjusted person?" "How does he get along with others?" "Does he have pet peeves?" "Is he easily threatened by others?" "Does he feel insecure?" "Does he want to dominate?" "Does he bring spiritual maturity to the group?"

With the right men and women, each meeting can be a blessing. With the wrong ones, it can be a pressure-producing hassle.

It's hard to be held back by the very people who should be your right arm of support, encouraging you and helping you to move ahead. A drag is always a strain, but when it comes from within your own ranks, you're not only frustrated: you are hurt.

The Beautiful People

God is in the business of making people good (Romans 8:29).

This means, that when you associate with godly people, you are sparing yourself many pressures and problems that you might otherwise encounter in your dealings with others. People who love Christ, love you. And you in turn can respond with all confidence because you are united in the bond of Christian love.

It makes no difference whether you've ever seen one another before, or if you even speak the same ethnic language: there is a kinship and a oneness when you are with others who share your relationship with Christ.

Russia is a godless country, and yet behind its wall of iron there are those courageous saints, undaunted by personal dangers who have committed their hearts to Christ. One of the most moving experiences of our lives was when we worshiped and fellowshiped with brother and sister believers in Moscow. Our verbal language was not understood, but we had no difficulty communicating through the language of the heart. We loved the same Lord, and we were welded together in His love.

Yet, even the godly, will at times disappoint you. As long as people remain on this earth, they are not impervious to Satanic attacks. Christians may fail you, but Christ never will. Others may let you down, but Jesus will lift you up.

So if you want to keep your people problems at a minimum, keep in the company of Christians but keep your eyes on Christ.

9. Money Matters Matter

It was late Saturday afternoon, and it *just had to be* one of the most wonderful days of Jim's and Caroline's life. They had just said, "I do" in the Chapel of the Bible college where they were graduating.

No reception had been planned because Jim and Caroline felt they would rather save their money for other things. So after the ceremony a few special friends gathered outside the Chapel to bid them good-bye as they were getting into their car and starting off for a weekend honeymoon.

"Oh, wait!" called one of the girls as she dashed out of the chapel. "Dean Smith and his wife sent you a wedding cake! It just arrived."

"Wonderful," exclaimed Caroline. "Oh! Isn't it beautiful? But—but, I don't know what to do with it. There are just the two of us, and we can't eat it all."

"Well, why don't we put it in the back seat," suggested Jim. "We'll surely run into someone who can enjoy it with us."

So they carefully placed the wedding cake in the back seat, and the couple drove away, all love and smiles—and virtually penniless!

They had scarcely gotten out of town when Jim said, "I don't know how far we'll be able to go, Sweetheart. We've barely enough money to pay for two nights at a motel, and about two dollars left over for gasoline."

But they just giggled and held each other's hand a little tighter and leaned over for an endearing kiss.

After about an hour, Jim felt they should pull into the next service station and get a little gasoline. As they did, they asked the owner of the service station how far it was to a certain city. "We're going to try to get that far. We've just started on our honeymoon."

"So you're just married?" asked the service station owner, jubilantly. "That's wonderful! How much gas? Shall we fill it up?"

"I wish we could, but I've only got two dollars, and we've got to get back to the Bible college Monday morning," said Jim.

The service station man looked at them rather quizzically and indicated that they were going to have to have more than two dollars worth of gas to get where they were going. Jim told him that two dollars was all he had. Then with a spurt of genius Jim said, "Say, I've got an idea."

He went back to the car and asked his bride if she would mind if he sold the wedding cake to the service station man so they could fill up the gas tank and have enough to go on. Caroline said that anything he wanted to do was "just fine" with her.

So Jim went back to the service station attendant and asked if he would like to buy their wedding cake so they would have enough money to get the gas. The service station attendant, somewhat shocked, said, "I don't want to take your wedding cake."

But Jim insisted.

"I tell you what I'll do," said the man. "I'll just *give* you some gas and that'll be my wedding present to you." So he put in five gallons.

The two happy lovebirds thanked him and drove on toward their destination.

As they were returning from their little honeymoon trip, they began to run out of gas again. And, of course, you know what happened—they offered to sell their cake! But each time they offered it, the service station attendant would give them a few gallons of gas. Finally they arrived back at the campus with a nice little two-day honeymoon—all on love and a few dollars! And they still had their cake!

You'd have to say two things about this young married couple: first, they were clever and resourceful; secondly, they didn't have much money.

You Can't Live without It

Needless to say, whether a person is single or married he needs some financial income if he is to ward off serious pressures in life.

Some people would say that the worst pressures in life are financial pressures. My daily mail would also suggest this. Of the thousands of letters that come to the headquarters of the Narramore Christian Foundation every month, many have to do with lack of finances. A wife will often write, "My husband doesn't make much money, and what little he makes he spends.

We're buying way over our heads. The bills are coming in and everything seems to be caving in on us. I don't know what to do!"

I often talk to men who say they've been unable to meet the financial needs of their families. Many households do not have needed medical attention. They are short on good food. They need clothes. They have no savings for rainy days. In a hundred other ways some families are suffering because of financial pressures.

Some financial problems rush in as a result of emergencies. A person may lose his job unexpectedly. Sometimes serious illness keeps a person from working, and brings on huge debts. A natural disaster such as a severe storm, earthquake or tornado leaves a family homeless and penniless. Many other emergencies can devastate a person's pocketbook, leaving him penniless.

Pressures of Our Own Making

Many financial pressures are of our own making. We bring them on ourselves. Often, as we look back and study the situation we have to admit that we caused the problem ourselves.

I remember so well a couple to whom I was giving premarital counseling. They were very much in love and wanted to get married. So they decided to have a few counseling sessions before they got married.

It was the second session, and we were working on a budget. Suddenly tempers began to flare. We discussed their income and expenses. I saw that it was going to be awfully tight. Finally, the young lady looked at her husband-to-be and said, "John, we just can't make it!"

"What do you mean?" asked John.

"Well, you can see for yourself we don't have enough money. We won't have enough to pay our bills."

The starry-eyed young man assured her that they would have enough. But she insisted they wouldn't. Finally, she asked him to show her just where the money was coming from. He muttered and sputtered for a few minutes, and she finally told him that she didn't think they should get married until they had enough income to pay their bills. He was very upset with this thought, but she stood her ground.

During the next counseling session they decided not to get married, at least not for a while. They put it off for almost a year. By that time the young man had finished college and had secured a steady job. This was undoubtedly wise planning. They studied their situation and found they didn't have sufficient income, so they did something about it. I'm sure it saved them months, and maybe even years of arguing, fighting, quarreling and complaining.

Balancing the Budget

Some people don't like the idea of a budget. But everyone has a budget whether he knows it or not. In talking with people, a wife or husband may say, "We don't have a budget." Actually, what they mean is that they have never sat down to determine what their income and outgo are. But everyone *does* have a budget. Everyone has expenses (and usually some income) whether he is cognizant of it or not. It's an intelligent couple that figures what their expenses are, and what their actual income is, then takes steps to bring them into line.

The Russells were a couple who were constantly in hot water financially. Sonehow they could never get around to developing a budget. Finally, between their credit card payments, their house and car expenses, and a host of other things, they were forced to do something about it. He decided to go to the Credit Union where he worked, and take a loan sufficient to cover all of their debts. This was taken out of his weekly check. The result was that the check was so small the couple had to skimp on their food to make their check reach.

If they wanted to take a weekend trip or do something special, he would have to work a second shift and earn some extra money to make it possible. This all added up to rigid discipline.

One day he said to his wife, "I've had it. I'm throwing all our credit cards away except one for identification. I'm not going to charge another blessed thing!"

Mrs. Russell liked his decision and agreed to go along with it. Before the baby came, however, she had to go to work to help with the coming expenses due to the loan commitment at the Credit Union.

If this couple had "counted the cost" before getting stuck in this financial jam, they could have avoided a world of pressure and strain.

Bert and Laura never felt the need for a regular savings plan. This "play it by ear" arrangement distressed Laura, because she knew someday an emergency would rear its ugly head, and they would not be prepared for it. Since the subject was touchy and usually led to a serious argument, she finally decided to take her hands off and let Bert do it his way.

Sure enough, an emergency came; and since they were not prepared for it, they had to borrow from the bank. But the payments proved to be too great a burden. Finally Bert suggested they make a budget and include a plan for consistent savings.

A Team Effort

I once knew a couple who were always having trouble with finances. It wasn't that they overspent, because neither of them believed in buying on time. Both had been brought up in homes where the policy was "everything down and nothing per month." And they practiced this rule.

The real problem was that the husband managed the finances entirely on his own, and he never wanted his wife to have anything to do with the checkbook. In fact, if she asked about the checking account balance, he resented it. He felt she was suspecting him of mismanaging the funds. In turn, she was upset with her husband because he hid all the financial matters from her.

"He thinks I don't have enough brains to handle the money," she thought to herself.

Actually he was an insecure person who felt he should hold on to the financial control. To let his wife work with him in the finances of the home would reinforce his feelings that he wasn't capable of managing matters. So he clinched this little corner of the family's affairs a little tighter.

This arrangement didn't work because the husband resented his wife's interference, and the wife resented the husband's refusal to include her on such an important part of their lives. Naturally they both lost out because they were always at sword's points with each other, and they lacked the good, clear thinking and planning of two people rather than one. In their home the management of finances became a severe pressure point which they never seemed to resolve.

A team effort would have helped this couple, just as it benefits *every* couple. Not only are two heads better than one, two heads tend to relieve the pressure!

Planning

If you should study one thousand families or individuals who were having serious financial problems, you would come up with some interesting findings. You would discover that most of the dollar dilemmas could have been side stepped if they had planned differently in the beginning. Intelligent financial planning begins long before a person reaches legal age. It starts when a person is just a child. All children need guidance from their parents and teachers. Even young boys and girls can understand basic facts about financial planning. Although youngsters are not involved in high finance, they can appreciate simple truths about income and expenses. Adults may give children a head start in life by helping them understand the value of money and basic principles of budgeting and saving. It's a wise parent who will help his child understand such things as wise buying, regular saving and thoughtful selling. This would start the child off into a thoughtful lifetime of budgeting, and it would save him mountains of grief and pressure over money matters.

Today there's a whole new ball game in planning finances. It is called *estate planning*. Like most people I hadn't given it much thought. But as the ministries of the Narramore Christian Foundation grew, we saw the need for men on our staff who would live in various parts of the United States and counsel with people regarding their income and their life's savings. Little by little we employed outstanding men for this responsibility; then we arranged for them to take the finest training possible. The organization that offered the training told me that as president of our organization I was entitled to take part of this training without cost. So I took advantage of this opportunity.

The picture soon became clear to me. Since the government needed huge sums of money, daily, to run its far-flung operations, it had to think up more and more ways to tax people. These taxes affected people while they were living as well as after their death.

I was amazed when I learned how much people could lose if they had not taken advantage of financial plans allowable by the government. I was also duly impressed when I learned how much nearly every person could conserve if, on the other hand, he had the proper knowledge regarding estate planning.

Indeed, *planning* is a key word in warding off financial pressures. But, unfortunately, many people never stop to make adequate plans.

Janice, for example, is a middle-aged woman who continually fights the battle of the budget. True, her income isn't great. But it is also true that she was raised in a home where planning was never practiced. And she will probably struggle along for years, not knowing what she's doing financially. But if she could be persuaded to start working out a simple plan of expenditures and income, she would eventually come up with some creative ways of making ends meet. The world is filled with people like Janice, whose financial pressures could be resolved, or at least lessened, if they would spend time planning their finances.

Psychological Aspects of Finances

It might come as a surprise to some people to realize that financial pressures are often psychological in nature. In general, actions can often be traced to feelings which people hold toward themselves. And actions that lead to financial pressures are no exception.

I know a woman, for example, who is typical of multitudes of men and women. She is intelligent, a devoted Christian, well-dressed, and has a pleasant manner and appearance. To talk with her at church or in your home or at a party, you may never suspect some of the deep feelings which influence her actions. But if you knew her innermost feelings you would realize that she harbors basic feelings of insecurity. She was raised in a home where her mother paid little attention to her. Her father did no better; he continually yelled at her and criticized her. During these crystallizing years of life she grew up feeling insecure and alone. Since childhood, nothing has happened to change these feelings appreciably. As a result, much of her behavior is based upon these attitudes which are hidden to most people. In fact, she is not aware of her feelings, herself.

A careful study of this lady would reveal that her insecurity shows up in her desire to have "things." She has a persistent desire to have more "things" in her house and especially expensive "things." Her husband doesn't understand her dynamics, but he does realize that she likes "very nice things." He also knows it drains the budget.

She is quick to notice what other people have in their homes. Then she wants similar things a little bigger, a little more expensive. Her closets are filled with clothes she doesn't really need. She wears a new outfit a few times, then she looks for another. This, of course, is a compensation. Unconsciously she is attempting to feel secure and appreciated by attractive "things." Her thirst for "things" is not limited to clothes. It goes in many directions. Needless to say, the family is under financial pressures, and the lady never solves her insecurity problem. *We never meet our basic psychological needs through devious means*. Your neighborhood, and mine, is filled with people who are trying to make "things" on the *outside* make up for what they don't feel on the *inside*.

With John Jones, it's a little different. A careful examination of his feelings would reveal the fact that he never felt loved. He was raised in a home of substantial financial means, but his father was busy making a living, and he spent little time with the boy. His mother was a quiet, cool person who seldom showed the boy affection. Little by little he grew up feeling that he was not worthy of love. Today, as a grownup, John goes on buying sprees. Unknowingly, he buys this or that to gain attention and admiration from his friends. He takes the family's money and spends it on some unusual article he doesn't need. But he feels that his purchases will bring attention and will cause people to admire him and like him. In other words, he is spending his money to buy people's affection.

Some years ago I worked as a psychologist on the staff of the Los Angeles County Superintendent of Schools. One day I was making a study of a boy in the fifth grade. As I worked with the boy, I learned that he was sneaking money regularly from his parents. What did he do with the money? He bought ice cream, candy and cold drinks. But strangely, he didn't eat these things himself. Instead, he gave them to his friends. He didn't care for the food especially, but he was trying to buy friendship. Down deep he felt he wasn't loved. He was a lot like John Jones.

Many budgets could be balanced if members of the family were well-adjusted, and not attempting to use money to compensate for their psychological problems. Several years ago I counseled with a lady who was exotically dressed, and looked as though she had spent several hours on her face before she left home. One day in counseling, she exploded, and screamed, "I hate myself, I hate myself, and everybody hates me."

This was the beginning of a whole series of insights for her. She was using exotic lotions, powders, face paint and the like, along with her extreme clothing styles because she felt inferior. She came from a poor family who worked overtime criticizing her. Also she felt she was from the wrong side of the tracks. Now, as an adult, she was trying to prove she *was somebody*.

This was in direct contrast to Sandra, the lady who lived next door to her. Sandra couldn't care less about dressing in the latest fashions and spending hours on her facial makeup. She had been raised in a home where her father cared much for her and showed her affection. Her mother, too, was a reasonable, loving woman. Consequently, Sandra had grown up feeling she was as good as anyone else. She had no need to spend money on trying to prove she was somebody.

The solution to these psychological financial problems is to realize that you have them. Then you can trace their causes and see just where they came from. It is important to realize that psychological maneuvering only makes the situation worse and puts a strain on an already flat pocketbook. The *real* solution is to focus on the *real* culprit: the emotional disturbance.

10. Conniving Competitors

When I took my first job as a licensed psychologist, I ran into some interesting experiences. During the evenings I often spoke to parent groups in schools and churches. One of the features of these meetings was the question-and-answer period.

After a year or so I saw that the questions always followed a similar pattern. Regardless of the community, the parents would come up with about the same questions. One subject had to do with *competition*.

What is the effect of too much competition in the schools?

How can you eliminate competition in the home? Or does it really matter?

Since a person is going to have to live in a world of competition, isn't it best for children to get accustomed to it when they're growing up?

Our son, Bob, comes home from school and says that he just can't keep up with some of the kids in the classroom. We tell him to forget it, but he says he can't. He gets butterflies in his stomach, and I'm afraid he's going to get ulcers. Do we *have* to have this awful competition?

And so the questions came, one after another, about the whole matter of competition. Some were for it, some against it.

God has planted in the heart of every normal person a desire to do better and in some way to excel. We not only see this in athletics but in every other field of endeavor as well. From the time a child is big enough to know that there are other children around, he wants to do things "bigger" and "better" and "faster."

This natural desire to move ahead and improve is wholesome. It provides incentive as well as fun. It adds interest and zest to life.

But competition becomes harmful when it interferes with a person's happiness, when the desire to "win" and "dominate" becomes more important than the activity.

An Experiment in Non-Competition

Shortly after graduating from college, I taught in an elementary school which experimented with a number of innovative ideas. One of these was the issuing of report cards without precise grades.

The principal, herself, was a relaxed, thoughtful person. She wanted each child to do his best without undue pressure from competition. Teaching in this school was a rewarding experience for me. Each month when the report cards were issued, teachers wrote a brief description of the child's activities and progress. But no grades were assigned. Frankly, I felt a little uncomfortable at first, not giving "A's" and "C's" or "1's" or 4's" or something in between. But as time went on I saw many advantages in this procedure. I soon learned, too, that the kids liked it very much. Some of the children who had grown up in that school had never received a "mark" and they didn't know the difference between an "A" and a "D". But they were happy, and relaxed, and they did excellent work.

But I noticed that when new students came into the school they sometimes had a rather difficult time adjusting to this "no grade" system and so did their competition-minded parents! For example, a mother who wanted her child to outdo all of the other kids would become upset when she learned that the students were not receiving grades. On a number of occasions I talked with mothers who had just brought their children into the school. These parents were not content unless their child was beating someone else out, trampling someone down, and getting all A's (or A-pluses). It would usually take several sessions to help such parents understand that extreme competition was not good for a child. It was a great joy to see parents finally gain sufficient insight to want to *relax*, and not keep their children under undue pressure because of too much competition.

The Last to Know It, but the First to Show It

Much of what people do is not on a conscious level. They just feel the way they feel, and the way they feel seems normal for them. This also applies to competitive feelings. A person may be reacting to what he feels or imagines is competition, yet not realize it. He may project his feelings onto others, or he may justify what he is doing, not realizing that he is overly concerned about others getting ahead of him.

You may even be highly competitive and not realize it.

This was Margaret's situation. She always wanted to do well, but she didn't realize that she lived in a world of "keeping ahead of people," pushing others aside and forcing herself up. Her attitudes had developed little by little through the years until it seemed perfectly normal to her to feel as she did. Without realizing it, she considered everybody competition. She was raised in a home where each person had to scramble for himself. The parents unwisely pitted them against each other and everyone else. The children even competed with their parents. In time, this became Margaret's way of living. She was continuously in competition with everyone, even in the smallest way.

At the same time Margaret was growing up, another child was raised in a nearby family. We'll call her Gail. In her home it was completely different. The parents talked and reasoned with the children. They tried to keep the children from being overly competitive. As a result, Gail grew up with a lot of appreciation and love for people, feeling that she, herself, was a worthwhile person. There was no straining every nerve every day, every waking hour, to try to get ahead and stay ahead of someone.

Margaret's emotional deprivations from childhood began to show up in countless ways as she became a wife and mother. She had many nagging problems which stemmed from her innate desire to compete. Although she was unaware of the dynamics, they bothered her just the same.

In her relationships with her husband she had a persistent feeling that she needed to "win." She wanted to be certain that he didn't get ahead of her. Margaret's husband never thought of her as needing to win. He just thought of her as being rather stubborn and having some hang-ups.

Margaret's persistent drive to get ahead showed up in church and everywhere she went. For example, when talking with a neighbor, the neighbor might mention the dishes which she and her husband had just purchased. Margaret could hardly wait until her neighbor finished talking so she could start talking about some of *her* dishes. Unknown to Margaret, she was telling her neighbor that she didn't want her neighbor to get ahead of her so she had to bring up something about *her* nice dishes.

Of course, Margaret's feelings of insecurity and wanting to get ahead of other people showed up in her dealings with her children. For example, she didn't like her children to get the best of her in an argument. She would argue, then a few minutes later she would come up with an additional point and start arguing again. Her dynamics inside would not allow her to give up and let the kids have the last say. On countless little occasions she tried to prevent them from getting ahead of her. Volumes could be written about her poor relations with acquaintances, her husband and her children.

Although Margaret didn't understand her own dynamics, she *did* know that "many people around her had hang-ups." In other words, she projected her own feelings onto others. To her, life was constant pressure because she could never afford to relax and be herself. Her inside compulsions turned everyone into conniving competition!

Winning over Your Competition

To eliminate the pressure of competition in your life, it is essential to gain insight about your own dynamics. You need to be aware of feelings which you may have about pushing others aside, or getting ahead of others and in general staying ahead of people.

But that's not all of the story. There's the "outside" part. It concerns the competitive environment in which you may work and live.

I remember talking with a fellow who was employed by a company that stressed competition. It was a sales organization that played one record, "Beat the Competition." Their administration devised a constant stream of pressures to insure more sales and to get in more money. Progress was built around squeezing the other fellow out of business. The owner of the company, himself, was highly competitive. He had an almost insatiable desire to move ahead of others. Little by little he gathered competitive people around him. Before long it was a highly aggressive, financially successful company, going about the work of pushing other people aside and cutting them down.

This particular fellow who was talking with me began to gain some valuable insights about his company. "You know, I think that working in this situation is bad for me. I'm already competitive by nature. But in this organization they have been honing up our competitive spirit to the point where it is unnatural. I'm competitive, yes, but I don't want to be pressured any more."

This man had begun to understand the unhealthy environment in which he worked—an environment which was reducing him to a competition machine.

It may be that you are in an environment where undue pressure is being placed upon you. If so, you should realize it and consider taking appropriate steps to correct it.

In summary, you will do well to look at competition from two points of view: *inside* as well as *outside*. Unconscious or hidden negative feelings may be prodding you on to a life of empty, devastating competition. On the other hand, you may be living in a little world of competitive people with competitive ideas designed to make money—and make you a pressure machine!

11. Flexing Your Muscles

"Hello, Joan." It was Steve's voice, and ten minutes before five o'clock.

"Oh, hi, honey," his wife responded. "What's up? Got to work late tonight?"

"Nope! I'm leaving this stuffy place in ten minutes, thank goodness! But don't meet me at the train tonight because I want to walk. O.K.? See ya, Babe."

"Must have had a rough day," Joan concluded as she hung the receiver back on the phone. Whenever Steve chose the twenty-minute walk from the commuter train in preference to the five-minute ride with her in their Rambler, Joan knew that her husband had wrestled with a pressure-packed day at the office.

"It's just this way," Steve had tried to explain after one of his *walking* times, "I feel so uptight when I leave that bloomin' office. I think I'm going to explode. But after I've walked that twenty minutes, I sure feel a lot better. I don't know why it works that way, but I know it does."

Steve was right. Physical exercise is a healthy vent for built-up tensions and pressure. How much better for Steve to "walk out" his frustrations instead of taking them out on his family.

The Pressure Build-up

If Steve hadn't "walked off" his pressure feelings, his emotional cork would have popped and he would have "blown off." That was the way Steve reacted to situations of stress. There are others, however, who attempt to ignore their frustrations. They don't want to talk about them: they want to forget them. But since they allow themselves no outlet for these bottled-up feelings, there's only one recourse: suppress them. TV, the easy chair, and sleep are often escape mechanisms for internalized hostility—the result of unresolved tension. A common complaint among wives is: "All he does is watch TV and sleep." It certainly does nothing to foster family relationships.

Typically, the "weary businessman" comes home from the office, eats his dinner, plops himself in front of the TV and sits for the rest of the evening. Quite often he dozes off while the TV continues to "do its thing."

But his wife can't quite understand this. "Why," she wonders, "is he so tired when all he does is sit at a desk?" She's been on the move all day: chasing after their toddler, cleaning up finger paint spilled by their preschooler, chauffeuring the older children to and from music lessons, marketing, vacuuming the carpet, ironing, mending, cooking, and a score of other physically taxing chores.

As for her husband, he may "sit at a desk," but that's not "all he does." He is working under the pressure of deadlines, job competition, a gossipy secretary, and—worst of all—a cantankerous boss who periodically threatens to replace him if he "can't produce the goods." Eight hours of that kind of pressure is enervating for even the strongest constitution. Little wonder, then, when evening comes and he finds himself in the shelter of his own home, he's "wiped out."

Escape Valve

What this man and his wife do not realize is that very few of the tasks we perform produce genuine bodily fatigue. Physical tiredness results largely because of the accumulation of metabolic wastes in muscles that have been overworked. But this condition is of short duration because your body is soon activated to carry off these and other toxic wastes along with them.

We are all aware that emotional and mental turmoil brought on by pressures and tensions can also produce fatigue. Your body's reaction to emotional stress differs from its reaction to physical stress in that fats are drawn from deposits, emptied into the blood stream, and deposited along artery walls. Too much of this, and you are in real trouble physically.

Physical stress is easy to control. When you're tired, you can stop. Not so with pressure or emotional strain. Such pressure remains to hang over you like a cloud and nag you. When the "weary businessman" switches on the

TV and goes to sleep in his chair, it is a subconscious effort to turn off the pressure carried home with him from work. This is a safeguard. A person can't carry active pressure with him every hour of the day, or he'll have an emotional breakdown. Unfortunately, because he "conks out" on his family night after night, it creates other pressures in the form of guilt. Now he has an added stress to plague his already pressured life.

If the "weary businessman," on the other hand, would pull himself out of his chair and force himself to do something physical rather than mental (watching TV is still mental, believe it or not), his emotional stress would be replaced by the immediate demands of the physical activity. Actually, he'll probably be less tired using his muscles than if he stays in his chair with his pressures.

Exercise as a pressure-reliever works for people of all ages in all walks of life. When Jimmy comes home from school, the first thing he does is hop on his bike. He wants to ride around for a few minutes because he's tired of sitting in a classroom using his head all day. He wants to pedal away some of the pressure before he starts in doing his homework.

Some years ago we needed some work done in the backyard of our home. The job entailed embedding railroad ties in an embankment that had been washed out in a rainstorm. It was heavy work, but yet it required someone with brain as well as brawn because, in a primitive sense, it almost resembled an engineering project. The Lord, who is interested in *all* our needs, put us in touch with just the right fellow for the job—Harry.

Harry was a student at a nearby seminary, working away on his Th.B. degree. Although his academic load was heavy, he needed money to meet his school obligations, so he was glad to take on the project. Each afternoon after classes were over, Harry swung the pick, dug post holes, and hoisted railroad ties into position along our back embankment.

"That's hard work, Harry," I empathized one day as I came by to view the progress of the construction.

"I know it," agreed Harry, wiping the sweat from his brow, "but it's great. After pouring over books on apologetics and Greek and what-have-you, it's great to get out of the library and do some physical work. School pressures can be pretty rough sometimes, but when I get out and exercise like this, it gets my mind off my studies and kind of clears the cobwebs of my brain. Sure, I'll be physically tired alright, but when I go back to the dorm tonight, I'll be refreshed mentally, and because of it, I'll be able to study better."

I was well aware that the school where Harry attended prided itself on its high academic standards. Many students were forced to drop out because they could not meet the demands or survive under the intense academic pressures. But Harry had found an escape valve—a release from the mental and emotional stress that conquered many of his classmates.

Mechanized Muscles

Another malady of our highly efficient, machine-made, civilization is what I call the "secretarial syndrome." Of course, I recognize that the remarkable technological advances of our twentieth century have ushered in a whole new world of amazing gadgets and labor-saving devices. Work has virtually been converted into knob turning, button pushing routines, and "thinking" has given way to computers. When it comes to conveniences and ease of living, we've never "had it so good."

But the "good life" isn't all that good. Its glittering plastic is empty and artificial, producing such malicious side-effects as pressure, tension and stress.

In years past, before society became so mechanized, everyone was a "do-it-yourself" expert. (There was no other way to do it.) Folks kept busy, but they had no problem finding their identity or accepting their place in the community. Thinking back to my boyhood, I remember how we used to get up before sunrise. The cock was our clock. We'd milk the cows, take care of the calves, feed the pigs, separate the milk, and by 7:00 o'clock we had worked up an enormous appetite for breakfast. After school there were more chores to do, like mending fences, doctoring cattle or butchering a pig. Then we'd get on our horses and bring the cattle into the corral. On typical Saturdays we repaired harnesses, mowed hay, threshed barley, irrigated crops, picked watermelons, and finished off the day in grand style with an old-fashioned ice cream social! No monotony, but a lot of muscle stretching.

What a contrast to the physical inactivity of today's urbanized society. Perhaps you are one of those who arises to the music of a radio-alarm clock. You swig down an "instant" breakfast while dashing to your fully-automatic, power-steered car. You snap on the car radio and listen to the news of the world, which is almost always depressing. On the freeway you stew and fret along with thousands of others who, like you, are bumper to bumper, inching along like a great metal snail, jammed on a grey asphalt track.

Once inside the concrete walls of the office, the deadly routine begins, and continues until clock-punching time at five. Oh, sure, there are coffee breaks and lunch breaks, but for the most part you find yourself doing the same thing in the same way, day after day, like a machine. You are glued to your chair (or you might as well be); your spine gets in position and stays that way. It's almost as though your feet and shoulders are locked in place. Then you fix your eyes on one little spot and push to get the job done, so you can start in again. No wonder your neck hurts and your head aches. People were never meant to be bolted down in one position. The body has joints and muscles which were made for movement. When you are subjected to this kind of punishment, day after day after day, year in and year out, you can count on being the victim of stress.

Maybe you dream of quitting the rat-race and settling down on a little place in the country—a simple cottage with a red barn, and chickens and cows and collie dogs. Others dream that dream, too, but for the most part, it never materializes. And so you're stuck in this tension-trap, trying to adjust to an unnatural environment.

Man in Motion

Although there is no panacea for the problems of our stilted, mechanized culture, there are some things you can do to counteract its ill effects. To prove that you're not a machine, try flexing your muscles. Snatch every opportunity while on the job to stretch, or stand, or move about. Use your lunch hour to do some walking, or even some exercise routines. At home, instead of watching TV or playing Monopoly, dig in the garden or paint the house. In this way, you will be converting destructive pressure into constructive energy. You may think you are too tired to tackle jobs like this. Remember, however, that your tiredness is largely the result of tension—both physical and mental. Think *exercise*, and you'll discover that physical activity helps to erase the stress while it renews your vigor.

Health clubs and gymnasiums, where specific exercises are programmed for your needs, are often helpful. The primary benefit derived from such an arrangement is that it *does* get you to exercise. Since you've signed a contract, you feel obligated to do your part and be there. Besides, you've paid in advance and you don't want to lose your money! For many, however, the added expense of a health club presents a barrier. But, of course, a person does not need a commercial organization to sponsor a program of exercise for him. It's just a matter of doing it, and really, for exercise, "there's no place like home."

Culture Change

Sometimes people shy away from exercise because of cultural inhibitions. They associate a program of exercise with physiotherapy or the "idle rich." During the past eight years, for example, more than a thousand ministers and missionaries have taken a month of specialized training in counseling at our international headquarters in Rosemead, California. In addition, hundreds of business and professional men and women have come for a week of intensive training in personal enrichment. Among the topics discussed, we specifically deal with pressure. But whenever we mention the value of exercise in warding off stress, invariably a certain number of these outstanding people will react in the same negative way. First, they feel guilty about taking time off from their busy schedules to play, go to a gym, or exercise in some other way. Second, they feel that exercising represents a different life style from the one in which they were raised, and that such "extravagance" would be a definite break with their past culture.

It is not unusual for people to feel this way. Yet, many of us live a very different life from those of our parents. The majority of our forebears "worked out" on farms or in fields from morning to night. Naturally, spas, health clubs, gymnasiums and exercise routines held little attraction for them. Twentieth century, sedentary man needs exercise, however, and shouldn't feel guilty about getting it. If he feels he's "too busy" to use the time in this way, he needs it all the more.

The Time Trap

Those who think that they don't have time for exercise are actually the ones who are caught in the tightest web of pressure. They may agree mentally that exercise is a good idea, but they always have "too much to do." Yet, if they only could realize it, the physical release of pressure helps them to get more done.

Al, for example, a hard-hitting middle-aged executive, didn't have much time for much else but "the Company." You know the type: he ate, drank and slept "the Company" because this was his whole life. Night after night, he took the problems and pressures of "the Company" to bed with him while he tossed and turned the hours away, fatigued but unable to sleep.

"Get ready for an ulcer or a coronary at the rate you're going," Al's doctor warned him.

Then one evening Al's teen-age son whose latest love in sports was tennis, challenged his dad to a game. In his younger days, Al had been quite a tennis enthusiast. Although at first he protested that he didn't have the time (there was usually "Company" work to be done at night), something about the winsomeness of the youth won out. Al consented to go "just this once" to show his boy how to *really* play.

To Al's chagrin, he discovered that his tennis form had gotten pretty rusty. He came home all "tuckered out," but emotionally relaxed and happy.

That night Al slept like a baby. "The Company" didn't even rate a dream. The next morning he felt more refreshed than he had for many months. In fact, the whole day seemed to go better because he *felt* better.

"If tennis does all this," Al chuckled, "I'll have to try it some more."

Al had made a great discovery—one that will undoubtedly extend his years. Exercise is an effective antidote for emotional turmoil and stress. It doesn't have to be tennis. It could be handball, swimming or jogging. Or even mowing the lawn. A long, brisk walk works wonders in blanking out troubled thoughts.

If you're one of the few whose job releases rather than bottles up pressure, you're probably not troubled with tension. I often think about Fred, a man who for years was in charge of our campus at the Narramore Christian Foundation. Although Fred was past the usual retirement age, he climbed up hillsides, planted trees, dug ditches, and didn't spare a muscle.

"It makes you feel good to exercise," he often said to me. "You ought to try it yourself!"

Well, I *have* tried it. And do you know, *it works*!

12. Helping Hands

Perhaps it's the rise of the ever-present ego that hoodwinks us into believing that we're indispensable. Or more likely it's the compelling threat of a basic insecurity that drives us to do it all ourselves.

Many of us subconsciously tend to associate the amount of our worth with the amount of our work. When we're overworked, we feel needed and important. The mere suggestion of help brings on a strong negative reaction, as though such an idea pointed an accusing finger at our competence. What's more, we fear the possibility that someone else might do the job as well or better than we do. In defense of our image we clutch our work all the tighter and wrap ourselves in its center. Yet, whatever the motivation or compelling force, the end result is the same. When we jealously guard our work loads and refuse the helping hands of people or machines, we seal ourselves into an airtight pressure-pocket.

Need Versus Help

Do you ever dream that you are running and running without making any headway? In such a frustrating dream, it's a relief to wake up.

In real life you may experience this same frustration. You work hard and long, but you see little progress. In fact, the work piles up faster than you can get it done. There's no escaping the problem, however, because you're not dreaming. It may be a nightmare, but it's for real.

When work gets you down and you feel discouraged because there's *so* much to be done, you are probably doing more than your share. This means that it's high time to let someone else help with the load. It's amazing how pressure will ease when you delegate a portion of your work to others. Assistance of this kind can boost your morale and prevent you from becoming depressed.

I once heard a busy woman say, "I know I can't do everything, but I sure try." She failed to realize, of course, that there's a double toll on overwork. It's not only hard on the worker; it's hard on the work. With the stress of an overload, something's got to give. Often quality is sacrificed for quantity. When you spread yourself too thin, you weaken your effectiveness.

The early church, with its phenomenal growth, began to experience a few problems along this line. Trouble was brewing over the mealtime routine, and who can deny that this wasn't a subtle trick of Satan in an attempt to keep the apostles too busy to preach. (Satan uses many devious tactics.)

The apostles didn't fall for it, however. Instead, they called an all-church business meeting and brought the problem before the congregation. "We should spend our time preaching, not administering a feeding program," they explained. "Now look around among you, dear brothers, and select seven men, wise and full of the Holy Spirit, who are well thought of by everyone; and we will put them in charge of this business. Then we can spend our time in prayer, preaching, and teaching" (Acts 6:2-4, *The Living Bible*).

There is nothing degrading about working on a lunch detail. In fact, those chosen for KP, as described in Acts, were choice servants of God and popular with the people. The work of "serving tables" was delegated to these men in order to alleviate the pressure which this job imposed upon the apostles. The new work arrangements gave the apostles more time to do the job for which God had called them, namely preaching, teaching and preparing by spending time in prayer.

Work needs to be shared, and God is aware of this fact. From the very beginning He knew that humans would need help from one another. It is true that Adam was alone at the first. Just why, we do not know. Perhaps God wanted Adam to realize how much he really needed another human being. We do know, however, that God recognized Adam's plight and put it on record that "it is not good for man to be alone." To remedy Adam's solo situation, God created "a helper suited to his needs" (Genesis 2:18, *The Living Bible*).

Since Eve was created specifically to be Adam's helper, it is obvious that God intends for human beings to work cooperatively. Evidently, Eve's job assignment was meant to take some of the work load from Adam's shoulders. Before Eve's arrival, Adam had no alternative but to care for the details of his work alone. He had full responsibility, and it was a big undertaking (See Genesis 2:15, 20). But when Eve joined the company, Adam's work was divided, and part of it was delegated to her.

Just because Adam needed Eve to help him, it doesn't necessarily follow that this arrangement formed a fixed pattern. Eve had needs, too, and Adam was there to meet them. Down through the millenniums of time, humans continue to rely on the help of their fellow men. God not only supports this plan, He commands it:

"Bear ye one another's burdens, and so fulfill the law of Christ" (Galatians 6:2).

Dare to Delegate

One morning during a coffee break, two administrators were discussing their work.

"Man," said Bill Knight, "I've got too much to do. I'm being plowed under. No matter how hard I work or how much I take home at night, I simply can't make a dent in that pile on my desk."

His friend, Dan, listened for a few minutes. He had heard Bill's tale of woe before. He had also heard what Marge, Bill's secretary, had to say.

"Poor Mr. Knight, he just works and works," she confided one day. "He never catches up. I'd really like to help him, but somehow he won't let loose. I'm sure I could relieve him of a great deal if he'd let me. But he never gives a project to me until it's almost finished. Then all that's left is just the typing."

So Dan put down his coffee cup and gently lowered the boom on Bill.

"Why don't you delegate some of those jobs to your secretary? Marge can handle 'em. Take the conference at Blue Lake, for instance. You could explain the project to her, and then the two of you work together and make a list of the twenty or thirty details that will need attention. Then turn 'em over to her and let her follow through. She'll do it fine. Marge could report back in three days, if you want, and this will give you a chance to check on her progress. Actually, you don't need to stew around with all that stuff. There's a lot Marge can do. She's a capable gal and she'll probably enjoy a little responsibility."

Dan's little lecture was what it took to shake Bill loose, and to shake his Blue Lake Conference loose, too. Together, Bill and his secretary, Marge, outlined the jobs to be done on the project, then established a priority list plus dates for accomplishing each item. A few days later Marge came back and reported her progress. Much to Bill's surprise, she had done just fine, and in fact, had even come up with some innovative ideas.

Bill soon learned that he didn't need to be so pressured at the office. He began to delegate rather than try to do everything himself. The result was that Bill and his secretary were both happier. He felt less pressured, and Marge welcomed the challenge.

Bill was fortunate to have learned this lesson. Many have not. Society is flooded with harried, overworked men and women who more readily accept an ulcer than share a piece of their work load. Tenaciously they cling to job details that ought to be done by someone else. Modern business men and women spend fortunes attending lectures, conferences and seminars where they are taught to let loose of work details that should be delegated to others. Perhaps the single greatest problem facing managerial personnel is that of *not* delegating responsibilities to subordinates who have actually been hired to handle them.

At our headquarters in Rosemead, California, the Narramore Christian Foundation offers a week of specialized training geared specifically to executives and business people. Significantly, the topic Delegating Duties is found to be one of the most helpful. Our trainees tell us that they experience a new freedom when they discover that they don't have to do everything themselves. For example, by delegating many routine, but time-consuming jobs, one executive shared how he was now able to utilize his time for more creative purposes. This is not meant to imply that one job is any more important than another, but it is necessary to recognize that a division of labor is both practical and efficient.

Dividing Your Duties

Delegating sounds like a simple operation, but there's more to it than meets the eye.

In the first place, be sure that the person you choose is capable of handling the job. Incompetency is difficult to tolerate. It can lead to nothing but frustration to all concerned. It could even prove disastrous, causing more work and trouble than you would have had without the "help."

To struggle over something in which one has had no training, or lacks all natural inclination, jeopardizes his emotional security and places him under a great amount of unnecessary stress. To put pressure upon the person who is working to relieve you of pressure, is both ironic and unwise. It's also unethical to reduce your stress at the expense of another. Furthermore, if the person to whom the work has been delegated does not feel confident or comfortable in doing it, he will require on-the-job training and supervision, or run the risk of turning out unsatisfactory work. Either way can be frustrating to you both.

Yet, well trained assistants are not always easy to come by. If the job you wish to delegate is of long duration or will be repeated in the future, it's worth training your own helper, if necessary.

Whether you choose an experienced worker or a novice, one thing is certain: *you* are the one responsible for the finished product. To avoid a bad scene in the end, you'd better paint a clear-cut picture now. You can't be too specific in your instructions.

The fact is, a common complaint among secretaries is that their bosses are too vague about what they want done. "You have to read their minds," one young secretary confided. But "reading" another person's mind is an art that few have mastered. In fact, the only really reliable "mind reader" is the God who created our minds. So, when giving a task to someone, make sure you know what you want done. If it's fuzzy in your mind, it will be fuzzy when you try to explain it to someone else.

So, when you're delegating a job to someone else, don't fail to spell out clearly just what you expect. Explain how you want the job done, and when it must be completed. Write your instructions so there will be no question about what you expect from your assistant. If you will take time to do this, you will eliminate confusion, avoid misunderstandings and the finished product should meet with your approval.

After you've turned the job over to someone who you believe is qualified and competent, leave him alone and let him work.

He's capable, and will do a commendable job without you breathing down his neck, continually checking on him. If you're going to do that, you might as well handle it all yourself, because you're not really delegating. This doesn't mean that you should be oblivious to his progress or withhold helpful suggestions. It does mean, however, that you must give your helper a vote of confidence and enough freedom to allow him to be his best.

Hiring a Helper

Sometimes all a person needs is someone or something to get him over the "hump." For example, you find that you are a slave to your house or your garden demands all your spare time. In all probability, it would ease your situation if you hired someone to help you. Perhaps a high school boy would like to earn a little money weeding your flower bed or mowing the lawn. And if you could have a lady do some housework once a week, or even every other week, what a great relief that would be. It might not even be a regular need. Perhaps it's only when you entertain that you feel the necessity for help. If you're having a special dinner party, it might keep your blood pressure from rising, if someone helped in food preparation or in washing the dishes. Your way of life determines your need.

You may feel that you cannot afford to spend money for extra help. Perhaps you consider this a luxury that you can do without. Yet, pressure is hard to endure, and stress makes living a strain. If by hiring a few "helping hands," you can relieve yourself of pressure and reduce the strain, would it not be a wise investment? Your personal well being is worth more than money.

There are times at our office when the staff is deluged with work. Although all of us are busy, the secretaries seem to feel the brunt of it.

"Why don't you bring in some extra help?" I suggest.

I have often explained to our staff that there's no need to struggle under a mountain of work. In our location there are numerous organizations that provide special secretarial help for short periods of employment.

"When you feel under the pressure of work," I tell them, "phone a secretarial service and employ a typist or two. They can assume a sizable work load and help get you out of a bind. If one or two days will take the pressure off, go ahead and employ them for that length of time. It doesn't cost much to get a little assistance, and it will ease things up for you."

Actually, an organization operates more efficiently and at no greater cost when its employees are not subjected to undue strain or tension. But more important than money is the health and happiness of the people who make up that organization.

"Helping hands" are not always of a human origin. The technology of our modern age offers a staggering number of labor saving devices which are geared to meet almost any imaginable human need. Many busy people find that these mechanical helpers lighten their loads. With less work, there is also less pressure.

Load lifters come in many forms, sometimes electronic. A lady I know was trying to write a book. She had good ideas, technical skills and plenty of imagination, but she was short on one thing: time. Although she could type (after a fashion), it was not her "thing." Typing out her manuscript was laborious and frustrating. Worst of all, it was time consuming. One day as she shared this problem with me, I suggested that she might find it helpful to use a small cassette with a built-in microphone. She could speak her ideas into the recorder, then give the tape to a skilled typist.

She was very grateful for the suggestion and latched onto the idea immediately. That very afternoon she went downtown and bought a small, compact cassette recorder. She carried it around with her and talked into it whenever she got an idea. She used it in the car while driving to pick up the children after school. She used it on her way to and from the market, and when she sat down for a little rest. She kept her cassette close by when cleaning the house or while doing the family ironing. Then, as ideas came to mind, she snapped on the switch of the recorder and talked to her "mechanical friend." Whenever a tape became full, she would have it typed. In just a short time she had completed several chapters. Now, writing had become a privilege instead of a pressure. Of course, because she dictated in snatches, there was always editing to be done on the first typewritten copy. For her, however, editing was a small price to pay for the convenience and the time saved by using the recorder.

There's no disgrace in "delegating" a specialized job to a specialized workman. A painter can paint your house; an electrician can install that new lighting system; a plumber is equipped to unstop that drain.

Sure, you can do it yourself. But if it results in stress and undue pressure, perhaps it's a better bargain if you don't.

The Do-It-Yourself Dilemma

To "do it yourself" is a popular concept these days. There are do-it-yourself books and pamphlets on every conceivable subject, and kits of every variety to help you do it. "Foolproof" instructions accompany these kits—and sometimes they prove that you were a fool for ever attempting such a complicated project in the first place!

If you have the time and enjoy a do-it-yourself challenge, go to it and more power to you. But if you are busy and time is of essence, or if projects of manual dexterity cause you frustration, you probably should let someone else "do it." When you "do it," you may save money, but you seldom save time. And if you're pressed for time, doing it yourself will undoubtedly "press" you even harder. If you don't have natural talent or know-how in the area of your project, it could even take a great deal longer—to say nothing of the stress resulting from your frustration.

Although home projects and do-it-yourself programs have their merits, one needs to evaluate his time and his ability. It isn't worth doing-it-yourself if it means unwarranted tension and stress.

It's a Family Affair

A small boy sat in the kitchen watching his mother busily prepare the evening meal. Since guests were expected for dinner, she was eager for everything to be "just right." As his mother hurried about, the boy was impressed that she was working hard.

"Mommie," he impulsively asked, "can I help you?"

"No, dear," she quickly replied, "I'm *too* busy for you to help me tonight."

Although the mother's answer may seem paradoxical, most adults can identify with her predicament.

In a paraphrase, the above story may have been told like this:

A mother was busy and could have used some help, but when her son offered, she refused his help, explaining that she was too busy.

Put like that, it takes on the characteristics of a riddle. But it needs no interpretation. I'm sure there have been times when you've felt pressured from overwork and would have welcomed a helping hand—except for one vital detail: the hand being offered couldn't do the job. In other words the only help available is unskilled and incompetent. We tell ourselves that we are too busy to train anyone else for the job. It's much simpler just to handle the whole thing yourself. So you continue to build emotional pressure as you continue to overwork, refusing to go to the bother of sharing your knowledge with anyone else.

This of course, is short-sighted. Naturally it takes time to train another person and supervise his activities. It also requires patience and understanding. You can expect to be slowed down during the training period. In due time, however, your "protégé" will have mastered the things that you have endeavored to teach him, and will be your able and valuable assistant. No longer a burden, he is now a blessing who helps to lighten the load that you once bore alone.

Many mothers, busy with the affairs of the home, make the mistake of not allowing children to help. "Run along and play," they tell their "younguns," "Mother would rather do it herself."

On the surface, this may seem indulgent. In reality, it's a disfavor to the child in that he never learns to do things.

A young bride, blushing with embarrassment, broke the news to her new husband that she did not know how to cook.

"But why *can't* you?" the groom asked in amazement, "I've eaten meals with you and your parents lots of times and your mother's a fantastic cook!"

"Sure," the poor girl tearfully replied, "Mom's a great cook. But she never allowed me to help her. She always said it was easier to do it herself. She never taught me a thing."

Of course, the bride could read, and with cookbooks available, in time she learned to cook. But the grim fact is, there are many brides who go through this same routine. Many times they go through life lacking self-confidence because they never learned to do things as children.

In another home, after the death of the father, the mother of four boys became the principal breadwinner and had to take a job outside the home. Although the boys were strong and healthy and old enough to have assumed a measure of responsibility, they never lifted a finger to help. In fact, they were shockingly slovenly in their habits, dropping clothes wherever they landed and strewing their stuff all over the house. In general, they turned the house into a disaster area. Then every evening the tired, harassed mother returned home and attempted to bring order out of chaos.

This shameful situation need not have been. Although it would have been difficult at first, had the mother trained the boys to take their share of responsibility and to help keep the house neat and clean, she would have saved herself much needless work and frustration.

A family is a cooperative enterprise. In order for it to run smoothly and efficiently, there must be a division of labor and every member must do his share. When anyone shirks his responsibility, the working balance is thrown off kilter and someone else must take up the slack. But when one person continues to be "stuck" with more than his share of the load, it creates tensions and strained relationships within the family circle.

Small children love to "help," and it's important that they learn to accept responsibility early. But when parents do all the work themselves, they are robbing their own children of the privilege of helping.

It's a good idea to reserve some little jobs for the little ones in a home. For instance, how about emptying waste baskets? Even a five-year-old can do that. Job delegation should start early. Of course, it must be a happy experience with lots of praise and encouragement. This is what makes work worthwhile.

It's amazing how much a family can get done when the mother and father take the time to teach their children how to work. The next step is to set up job assignments. Of course, parents will need to follow through on these to be sure that each task has been completed and is satisfactory. Children are capable of performing a great variety of duties which come in many sizes and types. Some jobs are appropriate for the very young, others are suitable for pre-teens and still meet the moods and abilities of teenagers. When parents sort out the jobs to be done and assign them according to age and ability, the family workload need not be heavy on anyone.

Not long ago I visited a home where a bulletin board held a prominent spot in the kitchen. On it was posted a list of various work assignments. When I asked about it, the father explained how it functioned.

"We divide up the work around here," he said. "We give the little jobs to the little people and the big jobs to the big people. We list the jobs right here on the board, and any time we find any job not being done (including my own) we require an accounting to the entire family. Most jobs are assigned for two weeks, then we review them. Some jobs continue for several months. It really works out quite well."

The man went on to tell me how before they started this "work distribution" program, his wife was always overworked. He also explained that pressure and tension had often resulted when disgruntled family members were asked to pitch in and work. Now there was never any question about what there was to do or who was responsible to do it.

"The kids really don't mind it, in fact they rather like it," the father told me as he summed up the explanation. "The best thing about it, though, is that work around our home is a family affair and we're all in this thing together."

Sharing or Shirking?

Although we've discussed the many benefits of delegating, it must be recognized as having a dangerous potential. Unless it is used with maturity and unselfishness, things that are *benefits* to you can be *liabilities* to someone else.

The purpose of delegating is not just to get yourself "off the hook" so you can take it easy while someone else does your work. That would be unethical. Such a system would be nothing more than an exploitation of executive privilege. Delegation used as a manipulative device for "passing the buck" is wrong.

I have known parents who have *used* their children in this irresponsible manner. By shifting their own responsibilities on the children, they were free to "goof off" while the kids waited on them and did their work for them like little slaves.

Of course, children *should* be given responsibilities and they need to learn how to work and help out as responsible members of the family. And sometimes there are extenuating circumstances where parents may be ill or suffer from physical problems. But it's a different matter when a strong, healthy father expects a son or daughter to take over his duties while he sits and watches pretty girls and old movies on TV. And it's a different matter when a mother sleeps till noon, day after day, while little tots struggle to care for themselves, or when she lounges on the sofa reading "True Love" magazines, expecting her children to scrub away on yesterday's lunch and dinner dishes. These people are abdicating their parental roles by letting their indolence take over. Children do *not* learn to accept responsibility in such negative situations. The fact is, a large percentage of what children learn is gained by example. But examples of this kind only serve to emphasize the advantages of a hierarchy. Just wait until Junior finds someone who is smaller than he is, and he'll begin a forceful series of his own "delegating."

There's a world of difference between delegating as a division of labor and dumping your responsibilities on someone else. Although others may not mind helping, they don't enjoy doing your work while you do nothing. They do not appreciate being *used*.

When work is divided, the pressure accompanying that work is also divided, and thereby lessened. But when you transfer the whole load into the lap of another, you also transfer the whole load of pressure. This kind of delegating is *not* sharing. Its real name is *shirking*.

Two-way Street

Some people seem to be "loners." Although they may not necessarily dislike people, they are introverted enough to prefer doing their own thing in their own way: alone.

When a "loner" finds himself weighed down with too much to do, he may walk away and forget the whole mess, or he may do it. Seldom does the thought occur in his antisocial mind that another person could help him. Work, he seems to feel, is one's personal business and not a thing to be shared.

Working as a "loner" has its place if you're wrapping Christmas surprises—or fulfilling a mission as a secret agent for the FBI. But in a cooperative society a "loner" is a misfit. People were made to interact, to share their blessings and their concerns. Yes, people operate at their maximum when they are supportive of each other in the areas of their need.

By allowing others to help us carry a part of our work load, we not only benefit from their assistance but, in a sense, we participate in a two-way sharing relationship. People are interested in projects when they themselves have a part. A delegated responsibility may be just what is needed to move a person from a comfortable complacency to active involvement.

Who knows, perhaps some day the picture will be seen in reverse. Your turn will come.

Yes, "helping" *is* a two-way street.

13. Recreation and Release

There's an old saying, "All work and no play makes Jack a dull boy."

This is more than just a saying. It's also true. No play not only makes Jack dull, it also makes him edgy and nervous, weighing him down with pressure. Rest and recreation started long ago, not with man, but with God. In the first chapter of Genesis, we read that God created the heaven and the earth. Then God went on to diffuse light. Then there appeared vapor and water, land and sea, plant-life, and the sun, moon and stars. God continued to work by creating all animal life, and finally God created man. All of this He did in six days.

After creating all these, the second chapter of Genesis says, "And on the seventh day God ended his work which he had made; and he rested on the seventh day from all his work which he had made. And God blessed the seventh day and sanctified it: because that in it he had rested from all his work which God created and made" (Genesis 2:2-3).

God was the first one to rest. And he wants you and me to rest, and to rest regularly. The human body was made to work, then to rest. If you *don't* rest, you'll meet with trouble. The body was designed in such a way that it cannot properly rebuild itself unless it gets proper rest.

One of the best ways to eliminate fatigue and pressure is to stop work and take it easy. The man or woman who doesn't rest sufficiently and regularly is not only punishing himself, he is also going against the clear teaching of God. And you know who'll be the loser!

Body Building

Each day many thousands of people are exercising and relaxing. Gymnasiums, health spas and other recreation centers are filled with men and women relaxing and re-creating. When rural life dominated the United States, the average man had no recreation center to attend; and he probably didn't need one. His work on the farm gave him all the exercise he needed. He was up in the morning, walking, running, bending, jumping, riding, and lifting from morning until night. But today's man is getting very little of this exercise on his job. He is sitting in one position, mulling over complex problems, worrying about the stock market, examining readouts from computers, and becoming more and more sedentary. He even feels embarrassed to run up and down the street in front of all his sedentary neighbors.

For most people, the twentieth-century life-style demands not only plenty of rest on a regular basis, it also urgently calls for various patterns of relaxation and recreation. It need not be the same for every person. What is recreation for one may be sheer boredom for another. For example, I would be bored stiff if I had to follow my wife around very long in a ladies' garment store, even though *she* "got the biggest thrill out of it." But hardware stores? Ah, they're different. I love to go into a large hardware store and see all the tools, implements, gadgets and the like. My wife may say, "What on earth do you do in a hardware store?" I really can't answer her. I just enjoy seeing and fiddling around with "exciting" items in a hardware store. If it's made of wood, or leather, or metal, I probably will like it! Such little treks get my mind off of other things, and give me a bit more perspective. It takes away the pressures of life.

Some people hesitate to set up a regular program of workouts at a gym. It's new for them and they feel a little uncomfortable doing it. Unconsciously they may be thinking, "My grandfather and father never did anything like this; and if they knew I was doing it they would probably think I had lost my marbles." But the chances are, Dad and Mom and Granddad didn't live the sedentary life you are living. They didn't need it, but you probably do.

Devices for Diversions

Many people have their own "do-it-yourself" plan. They swim, ski, hike, ride, do push-ups and a host of other things that give them exercise and a change of pace. Some men and women are wise enough to give special attention to their sleeping habits. Some have regular sleeping hours with additional sleep on certain nights, or naps during the day or early evening. Regardless of the plan, you won't feel nearly so much pressure if you set up a regular program for resting, sleeping, relaxing and re-creating!

I'm always interested in people who write me and tell about their off-duty activities. One man wrote recently about his organ accomplishments. He was a carpenter, but he decided to get a used organ and take lessons. Although it was strictly an after-hours project, he evidently did very well. In fact, he began specializing in hymns appropriate for memorial and funeral services. In time he started recording his music and sending tapes to funeral homes. Much to his surprise they paid him well for his tapes. The last I heard from him, he was sending his organ tapes around the country and making almost as much from his hobby as from his regular job. And, of course, he enjoyed every minute of it!

I remember a secretary who broke her routine by making miniature leather saddles. She got so good at it that she began featuring them at leather stores. "Now, I've got myself into a real pickle," she wrote. "I'm having so much fun, and doing so well financially that I'm tempted to stop working and devote full time to playing."

The world is an exciting place with exciting people in it. But many of them never learn how exciting things are or how interesting they, themselves, are. They get bogged down in daily routine and fail to discover their "genius." And even more, they load upon themselves tasks and routines which fill their lives with pressure.

Change of Pace and Change of Place

Another way to handle pressure is to escape to a change of scenery. Getting away even for a few hours does a world of good. You don't have to make a big deal of it, or go to much expense. It can be in the form of a picnic, a ride, an overnight stay, a visit to the zoo or beach or mountains or desert. Almost anything to get away and get your mind off your pressures.

Pressure is brought on, in part, by monotony and routine. Your body was never intended to be a machine. But that's what many of us are: machines doing the same *thing* in the same *way* at the same *time* with the same *people* at the same *place*. But when you break the monotony of the shop or office you feel differently, and tenseness begins to disappear.

I know a family that has found this secret. They are always planning and taking little jaunts. They pile into their car and start out someplace. Before long they're in another location having some new experiences. When they come back home they are happy and excited, and sometimes tired! But they've had a change of surroundings. But poor Mr. Long who lives next door to them has stayed home, done the same thing and piled up more tension and pressure. He lives alongside a family who has learned to break the routine, but the Longs have never been able to break out of their mold.

It's a welcome release to drive a few miles, have a change of scenery, then come back and start to work again. Simply being with new people and seeing new places is helpful. Your mind is flooded with new thoughts. You gain a better perspective. Threatening things seem to shrink to their actual size. You see new ways to handle situations. In a sense, you are a new you minus pressure!

14. Talking Away Your Tensions

"He's the strong, silent type," the sweet young thing rationalized while attempting to explain her introverted fiancé. What she really meant was, "He's not very communicative. I don't know what he's thinking, so I presume that it must be an indication of strength."

If the truth were known, a more accurate interpretation of his silence might read: "There's a lot of pressure pent-up inside, and I'm afraid to open the escape hatch."

A *quiet* person may give the outward impression of calm and composure, but trapped inside may be bottled-up tension and emotional turmoil that are seething and boiling.

Made for Talking

God never intended for human beings to "keep it all in." In creating man God gave him a mouth, a tongue, vocal chords and all the other equipment for talking. Then God started talking with Adam. God communicates with us in a myriad of ways. He tells us his feelings: He abhors sin, but loves the sinner. In His Word (the Bible) He shares with us His eternal plan and assures us of His everlasting love. What is more, God created us in His own image which means that we, too, have a capacity for the expression and sharing of ourselves. He intends for us to do just that.

There are various ways in which people can communicate. The most effective, of course, is through speech. Through words we are able to express our deepest thoughts and highest emotions. In Matthew 12:34 and Luke 6:45 we read, "Out of the abundance of the heart, the mouth speaketh."

Speech serves a kaleidoscope of purposes. By talking, you get across ideas, relate experiences, express your feelings, instruct others and ask questions. Words enable you to pray, to ask, and to thank. They are the audible expression of your inner self. But one of the primary benefits of verbal expression is that it serves as an emotional catharsis. God has ordained this method to help you rid yourself of pent-up tensions. Serving somewhat the same purpose as an air valve on an inner tube, talking permits your pressure to escape: it brings release.

Of course, there's the incessant talker who continually "runs off at the mouth" and gets on your nerves. But unknowingly, he may be practicing self-therapy. Since he doesn't harbor his feelings, he gets them "off his chest." By unloading himself he releases inner pressures which he might otherwise not be able to handle. If it were not for his ability to "spill it all out" by talking, he might eventually become very disturbed, possibly requiring hospitalization. Emotions and tensions which are sealed up on the inside tend to ferment, creating even greater pressure.

The Pressure-Releaser

A woman, complaining about her taciturn husband, remarked to a friend, "Talking to him is like talking to a wall. He's so unresponsive that in my frustration I vow I won't talk either. But then I become doubly frustrated, because I really *need* to talk."

She hit the nail on the head. We *all* need to talk. It's a universal *need* inherent in man's very nature. People who are unable to express their feelings by communicating with others are vulnerable to emotional and mental disturbances. Human beings *must* talk and air their feelings in order to maintain normalcy.

Mary impresses others as a very friendly person. She knows no strangers and has no inhibitions when it comes to talking. But after people get to know her, they realize that Mary has deep emotional conflicts. Underneath a charming exterior, she bears the scars of emotional deprivations stemming from her formative years. The basic needs of love, acceptance, and a sense of self-worth had never been met. In her childhood, her parents had underscored their rejection of her by chronic criticism and condemnation. She was never made to feel important, not to them or to anyone else. Now, as an adult, Mary unconsciously bids for the acceptance that she never knew as a child. She is intelligent and unusually pretty, but it does not alter her low self-esteem. Because she has never felt accepted, she cannot afford to accept herself. Mary is willing to admit that she has a few problems, but she does not understand the depth of her maladjustment nor the dynamics which have worked to produce her poor self-image.

Feelings of inadequacy create pressure situations in *any* setting, but when those feelings are submerged beneath a layer of years, they become difficult to decipher. We can more easily accept the things we see and understand. *It's when pressures bear heavy without any apparent reason that they are difficult to handle*. Mary, however, has found a way to compensate. Although she is unaware of the dynamics at work in her personality adjustment, she has discovered that she is happiest when she is talking. It makes her feel better. Mary says it's because she "loves people," that she wants to be around others and "talk" with them. Actually she is incapable of liking others very well, because her own negative ego-image does not allow her to like herself. But she seeks out people to whom she can talk because talking brings relief. Much of her strong feelings and her consternation are vented in this way. For Mary, talking is the escape valve which releases enough internal turmoil to permit her to function in everyday life.

Unfortunately, her relief is only *temporary*. Since her talking is not structured toward overcoming her basic problem of a low self-image, it does not absolve her pressures. True, it alleviates them to some degree. But since talking does not change her feelings of inadequacy, she still has her problem, and inner tensions continue to mount. The result: Mary keeps talking in order to relieve enough pressure to continue functioning in a normal fashion. The kind of talking needed to resolve such deep problems on a permanent level would require structured counseling by a trained therapist over a period of time. Like thousands of others, she too, could get help.

Although our "hang-ups" may not be as deep-rooted or as serious as Mary's, we all have pressures that can be alleviated through the age-old method of talking. By discussing even "little bitty" concerns, it smooths away nagging edges that could cause us to feel tense and irritable. When we talk about a distressing situation, we are actually thinking about it and sorting it out. Often this is enough to help us see where the pieces should fit together, and thus enable us to solve our problem.

A Confidant

Looking back over the history of the United States, we know that nearly all of the Presidents have had their "kitchen cabinets." In other words, there were those who held no official government position, yet were such close friends of the chief of state that he would share and discuss his plans and his progress with them. Every President has had certain people with whom he felt close enough emotionally to share his personal thoughts, his dreads and his dreams.

It means much to get your feelings on the outside and share them with a confidant, someone emotionally close enough to care. It may be an associate, or your wife or your husband. It might be a friend, someone who will guard in confidence those things that you have told him; someone with whom you can share openly and freely.

The very best confidant and friend that a person can ever have is our loving Heavenly Father. God wants us to verbally share all our pressure problems with Him. Not only does He have the ability to do something about them, but it's His plan for us to communicate with Him in this way. Have you ever thought about it? God knows everything about us, and when we tell Him about our needs, we are not feeding Him any new information. We are, however, learning to accept Him as our close friend. By talking with Him, we are learning to know God in a deeper, more personal way. He clearly instructs us through His servant, Paul, that we should "be anxious for nothing, but in everything by prayer and supplication with thanksgiving let your requests be made known to God" (Philippians 4:6, NASB). When we talk to God about our pressures, the result is that "the peace of God, which surpasses all comprehension shall guard your hearts and your minds in Christ Jesus" (vs. 7). What relief! Peace surpassing comprehension! Why we don't talk to our Heavenly Father and appropriate this peace is sometimes hard to understand. Joseph Scriven aptly expressed our tragic foolishness in the words of a beloved hymn:

"O what peace we often forfeit,
O what needless pain we bear,
All because we do not carry
Everything to God in prayer!"

Person to Person

God's plan for man, however, is more than vertical. To know Him completely, we must know Him in every dimension. On the horizontal level, His perfect plan is that we should "bear one another's burdens, and thus fulfill the law of Christ" (Galatians 6:2).

If you are wondering why God expects us to unburden ourselves to anyone besides Himself, think back to the way God made us. If God had only intended for us to have a vertical relationship, Eve would not have been necessary. But God knew that it was not good for "man" to be alone, and that also included women. He knew that people needed the love and support of other people, that they needed to "bear one another's burdens." This is God's arrangement, and it works. It is in His plan that we extend a helping hand, lend a listening ear, as well as share of ourselves and our burdens.

The reciprocity of a sharing relationship is a must within the body of Christ. God shows us clearly that no part of the body is independent of any other. The Apostle Paul wrote in 1 Corinthians 12:25-27, ". . .there should be no division in the body, but that the members should have the same care for one another. And if one member suffers, all the members suffer with it; if one member is honored, all the members rejoice with it. Now you are Christ's body, and individually members of it."

Jeopardizing the Image

But sharing of ourselves is not easy, for when we admit our pressures and concerns, we leave ourselves vulnerable. Rather than jeopardize our "image," we may find ourselves unwilling to reveal our needs. And so we stubbornly resist the help we so desperately need while we stagger beneath the crushing weight of emotional pressure. We are no better than emotional phonies as we go limping along, pretending that everything is alright. We don't want anyone to know that there are nagging fears and concerns which haunt us day and night. We wear bright-colored masks and smile while others admire our "ideal" situation. Never would we want anyone to know of the hurts we harbor or the heartaches we hide. So we hang a sign on the outside of our lives that reads, "Business as usual," while the very foundations are being gnawed away by tensions and stress.

Why do we hug our burdens to ourselves and refuse to let others share in the load? Why are we often so reluctant in unburdening our hearts to someone else? Why? It goes back to our basic feelings about ourselves. We shy away from talking to someone about our problems because we are afraid we will "look foolish," or we fear that we may be misunderstood. We don't want to risk the chance of revealing ourselves for fear of incurring the disapproval or losing the high esteem of our friends. We also hesitate in the fear that we may be blamed for creating the situation in which we find ourselves. To be told that "it's your own fault" is too much to take when already taxed with tensions and struggling against stress. When disapproval is expressed through blame or any form of rejection, it suggests failure and this becomes an additional pressure. Instead of the burden becoming lighter as a result of having shared it, we are saddled with even more pressure than we carried in the first place. Although it's rough to bear the strain of burdens alone, it may seem safer than risking the chance of rejection by the one from whom we seek help.

The story of Mike's frustrations illustrate this point. For some time he had been bragging about his expected promotion. When Higgins, the "big boss," retired, everyone would step up a notch. For Mike, the promotion would be especially meaningful since it would place him in a position of considerably more responsibility with a much higher salary. In fact, he had already put in his order for a new, expensive "prestige car," one that would be "fitting of his new role in the business world."

But Mike was in for a gigantic letdown. When Higgins retired, some of the personnel moved up, but Mike remained in his old job. Filling the place that Mike had thought would be his, was an "upstart" from a branch office who turned out to be the son-in-law of the vice-president. Mike rankled under the injustice of the move, and bitterly resented the usurper of the job he felt should rightfully have been his. Because of Mike's disgruntled attitude, from the very first, he and his new boss rubbed each other the wrong way. They clashed on every decision and Mike soon found himself threatened with the possibility of losing his job.

With pressures like these, Mike needed to talk to someone who would listen and give him encouragement and support. He should have shared his strong feelings and hurts with his wife, but instead he told her as little as possible. "She'll think I'm the biggest flunkie that ever lived," he reasoned. "I don't want to tell her any more than I have to."

Why do you think Mike refused to share the burdens of his job with his wife? What was he afraid of? Did he fear that she might accuse him in some way of gross inadequacy? Or, could it be that he felt she would nag him to get in and fight for his rights—an action that Mike knew would prove futile—and probably fatal? (It could even have been that his wife was a gossip. Mike didn't want his "failures" aired to the community. This would be too humiliating.) If his wife had been a godly woman who was accepting and understanding, she could have encouraged Mike to talk out his frustrations and his disappointments. By discussing his feelings of resentment and his anxieties, Mike could have resolved much of the emotional turmoil that plagued his daily living. He might not find himself elevated to the next income tax bracket, but he would at least be happy and contented in the Lord.

It means so much to have a friend or a loved one who doesn't tell you what to do, but rather, *encourages you to talk*. Most of the time you don't need answers; you need to be heard. The questions you ask are often bids for the chance to talk yourself. Talking helps you to bring your frustrations and concerns into the open where you see them as they really are and can deal with them in a realistic manner.

When the Hurt is Deep

When a burden weighs heavily upon you, talking becomes extremely important. Naturally, you're not going to share it with someone you feel is inadequate to handle it, or who doesn't seem to care. Another deterrent in sharing a problem can be a sensitive nature. You are embarrassed to air your troubles before someone else. Or it may be hurting so deeply that it's too painful even to discuss it. But if we are to find any relief from such a stressful situation, we *must* talk about it.

Jeff was only thirteen when he heard the traumatic news that his parents were getting a divorce. His father was too much of a coward to tell Jeff himself. One Friday his dad quietly moved out of the house while Jeff was at school, and that was the end of that. It was up to Jeff's mother to break the depressing news. So when Jeff came home from school on that fateful Friday afternoon, she sat him down in the living room and with bitter tears, related the hard facts to her son. She then told Jeff that as far as she was concerned, his father had ceased to exist. She made it plain that she did not even want his name mentioned. "It's a closed chapter," she explained. "We must forget about him and make a new life for ourselves."

But for Jeff, this was quite impossible. To erase the emotions and memories of one's entire life—especially when it's *not* of your choosing—is easier said than done. Jeff's world was shattered. He couldn't really take sides because he loved both mother and father. He knew that there had been wrongs, but he could see them with unbiased eyes. It wasn't a one-sided problem. Since he wasn't married to either one, he could be more objective. He could see where both parents had been right and where both had been in error. The court decided that Jeff be awarded to his mother, but his heart remained divided and torn between both parents.

The pressure of Jeff's emotional turmoil was doing terrible things to the boy. His school work fell way down and he became morose and touchy about even little things. He desperately needed to talk to someone who would listen and encourage him to sort out his bottled-up feelings and anxieties. To talk with either parent, of course, was impossible because they were the core of the problem. Other relatives were not very objective either, since they only knew the side they had heard. To share his feelings with peers was not the answer either. They were too immature to be of much help. He could have talked with his Sunday school teacher, but Jeff was much too sensitive about the whole sad scene to let anyone know how badly he was hurting. So he kept in all in and suffered through the most miserable years of his young life. Naturally, he was left with deep emotional scars.

Repress and Distress

To repress pressure by plugging up the escape valve is to ask for problems. Pressure has to go somewhere. If it isn't released through the channel of verbal communication, something else will give. Unfortunately many people are not aware of the damage they cause by sealing up their God-given emotional vents.

When Marcia, a woman in her early fifties, suddenly lost her husband, Jon, through a tragic accident, her world fell apart. It was true that both Marcia and Jon loved Christ and were active in their church. She knew her beloved partner was with his Lord. But Marcia was very dependent, and her life had revolved around her husband. Now her world had become confused and empty. They had no children and no close relatives. Her husband had been a strong leader and had handled all affairs of business while Marcia took care of the home. The thought of facing the world alone, making all the decisions, taking care of finances and a thousand other details overwhelmed her.

After the initial shock and a period of numbness had worn off, Marcia went through a time when she wanted to talk. But her well-meaning friends did not understand that by talking she was fulfilling a need. To "help" her they firmly told Marcia to think of other things and not to keep talking about Jon. When tears would start to flow, they reprimanded her and admonished that she should exert "self-control." Marcia choked back the tears and sealed her mouth as thoughts of Jon flooded her mind and pulled at her heart. Her advice-giving friends were happy because they had "helped her," when actually Marcia had simply internalized her grief. What they didn't know was that it was destined to appear again, perhaps next time in the form of an ulcer.

The best way to become agitated, upset and pressured is to keep everything inside. God knows this. That's why He intends for us to talk and to share our concerns and anxieties with others who care. But when we find an unfriendly door mat, or pull into our shells like clams, or refuse to face ourselves in an effort to protect our false pride, not only do we ignore God's commands; we sin against ourselves as well.

There are penalties to pay when we refuse to talk. Repressed pressure may take its toll along various roads, but a very common disorder brought about by bottled-up feelings is depression. By a process of emotional metamorphosis, pressures and tensions that are never vented or given release can change into internalized hostility. A common form of depression is one in which its victims harbor hidden hostility. When we learn to talk things "out," it helps us find a solution. Things that are kept on the inside cannot be handled, but *those which are brought out in the open can nearly always be handled*. We sense much less pressure when we talk out our concerns.

A Listening Ear

We've seen that many people have too little understanding or too many "hang-ups" of their own to act as good sounding boards for someone else's problems. Not everyone has a gift in counseling. Not everyone has even the ability to listen. Relief from the pressure of problems or pent-up emotions doesn't happen by listening to a lecture as much as by doing the talking. But few are disposed to listen. They much prefer talking. In fact, unless they offer advice or tell about themselves, they are prone to consider their time as wasted.

Finding a suitable confidant—a person to whom you can express your feelings and share your needs—is extremely important. Perhaps a good guide in seeking out such a person is to measure his qualifications against those set down in God's Word for church leaders. He may or may not consider himself a leader, but even if only an audient friend, he still exerts an influence. It is imperative that we take our cues from the right people. In the sixth chapter of Acts, the third verse, we read that the disciples chose men for serving on tables who were "of good reputation, full of the Spirit and of wisdom." If God considers it important to have people of that caliber for simply waiting on tables, I see no room for leniency in the choice of a confidant. Yet there are many who indiscriminately tell their troubles and frustrations to anyone who will listen. This is dangerous business because they are likely to get unsound advice, which if followed, would only compound their troubles.

When looking for a listening ear, there is one requirement that precedes all others: As Christians, we are to seek our counsel from the godly, and not from the godless who either consciously or unconsciously seek to destroy us. The opening words in the book of Psalms advise that happiness and contentment are *not* to be found by following "in the counsel of the ungodly" (Psalm 1:1). The remainder of the Psalm is an eloquent comparison of the divergent ways of the "godly" and the "ungodly." The final verse summarizes the discourse by declaring that "the Lord knoweth the way of *the righteous*, but the way of the ungodly shall perish" (Psalm 1:6).

Those of us who have accepted the provision of God's Son, paid as the penalty for our sin, are "the righteous." We become that because our lives are now "in Christ." All redeemed Christians are part of His "body"—the "body of Christ." *We* are the ones whose responsibility it is to bear the burdens of "one another." But as for those *outside* of Christ, how can we expect them to understand our needs! Since they are not in God's family, it's impossible for them to see our problems from God's point of view. Naturally, the solutions they offer are limited to the thinking of the unregenerate and lacking in godly wisdom.

The burdens of a Christian are meant to be shared with others of "like precious faith." This, of course, does not absolve us from the responsibility of being a Good Samaritan to the unsaved. In other words, we can and should reach out to help those who do not know Christ. This is one way in which we can demonstrate the love of God. But the unregenerate is incapable of understanding our personal relationship to Christ. He lacks discernment and is not qualified to "bear our burdens." We live on separate planes.

If you do *not* know Christ and need to talk with someone about the pressures and problems that are crowding your life, you, too, would be wise to seek out a Christian. Although, as stated above, Christians and non-Christians are on different planes of reference, those who are in God's family are on His level, which is higher and wiser than man's. The Christian can bring you to Christ, and you, too, can be in God's divine field of reference.

Among the qualities to look for when seeking out a confidant is an exemplary Christian life. This doesn't mean that he's perfect. That is an impossibility. But you do want to make sure that he isn't worse off than you are. How can he help you if he's messed up himself? God says that his life must be "above reproach" (1 Timothy 3:2). He should also be gentle, thoughtful and kind. With sincere Christian love, he should accept you as you are for yourself, but without condoning wrong actions. He should be peace-loving and friendly. He should also be self-controlled, discreet and prudent in all he says and does. The third chapter of 1 Timothy describes these required characteristics and many additional ones. It is a foolproof guide:

An overseer, then, must be above reproach, the husband of one wife, temperate, prudent, respectable, hospitable, able to teach, not addicted to wine or pugnacious, but gentle, uncontentious, free from the love of money. He must be one who manages his own household well, keeping his children under control with all dignity (but if a man does not know how to manage his own household, how will he take care of the church of God?); and not a new convert, lest he become conceited and fall into the condemnation incurred by the devil (1 Timothy 3:2-3, NASB).

A Friendly Neighbor

It has been said that more counseling goes on over the "back fence" than in the counselor's office. Today the "back fence" often takes the form of a telephone. A person feels frustrated, or upset, or misunderstood! He reaches for the phone and talks about his gripes to a sympathetic friend. If your problems are not too involved, and if the individual possesses the majority of the qualifications listed above, your back-fence friend or phone confidant may be just the one to provide the support you need to carry you through your emotional crises.

Sometimes, however, our problems are deeper than we realize, or than we want to admit. On the other hand, we may be well aware that the situation confronting us is serious, but we are stymied as to what we should do. Complicated, deep-rooted problems are not fitting material for a back-fence quorum. In such cases it is wise to have a talk with your pastor or to seek out a qualified Christian counselor who has been trained to help people with serious problems such as yours.

There is an ancient Babylonian proverb which makes the bold claim that whereas "speech is silver, silence is golden." I will grant that there are times when silence is more eloquent than words. When such is the case, silence also speaks—but in a language all its own. Yet, when speech becomes the magic key that can unlock excessive pressure and relieve pent-up emotions, it may still sound like silver, but its heart is forged of gold!

15. It's in Your Head

Ben Johnson once said, "Ease and relaxation are profitable to all studies. The mind is like a bow, the stronger by being unbent."

Most of us would agree that it is important to relax, but we don't always know how to go about it. I remember an experience I had once with the whole theme of relaxing. It occurred when I was serving as a psychologist on the staff of the Los Angeles County Superintendent of Schools. There we had a large staff that served on various committees. As chairman of the Audio-Visual Committee, I reviewed all of the films and recordings which were sent on consignment to our Department of Research and Guidance.

On this particular day, our division secretary said, "Here is a new recording which has just arrived. I presume you'll want to listen to it to see whether we should buy it or recommend it for use in local school districts."

I thanked her, took the recording to the audio-visual room, and looked at the label. Much to my surprise, the title of this long play record was, "How to Relax at Any Time."

"Well, that's interesting," I thought to myself, "I wonder what it's all about?"

So I put it on the record player. The narrator, I noticed, was Miss Sally Jones (or some other such name).

I forget her exact words, but Sally Jones started something like this: "How would you like to learn to relax? To relax anytime, anywhere?"

"Fine," I said to myself, "that's okay with me. Let's see how I'm supposed to do it."

So Sally went on. She explained, convincingly, that most people were uptight even more than they realized. Then she added that we didn't have to go through life so tense. So she would teach us how to *really relax*.

The next thing that caught my attention was the promise that she was going to relax all of my body.

"I'm going to start with your hair and scalp," she said. "Then I'm going to go all the way down to the soles of your feet."

I thought this was rather interesting and I began to wonder just how she was going to manage my liver and pancreas! By this time I was beginning to think I was a fool to waste my time listening to such trivia. But I decided to give Sally a few more minutes to see if anything would really happen.

Surely enough she started with my hair and scalp. She said that I probably had more tension in the top of my head than I realized, and she suggested various facial grimaces and movements of my scalp to get that part of me loosened up.

Then, little by little, she started on down toward my toes. She talked about my neck and shoulders. Before long, and much to my surprise, I was enjoying this relaxing exercise.

About an hour later, when I went back to my office the head secretary asked me how I liked the recording on "relaxation." I looked rather startled and said, "Well, I really don't know. You see, after a few minutes I went to sleep and I didn't get to hear the rest of it!"

We both laughed and decided that it must have been very successful.

From that day on I realized more than ever that human beings do get themselves into some pretty bad fixes during the day. For example, you can be riding along in your car. It wouldn't be so bad if you weren't in a hurry or if there weren't anyone else on the road. But that's seldom the case. You're usually rushing and straining every nerve and muscle to get somewhere. In addition, you're fighting traffic, seeing if the woman on the right is getting ahead of you or if the man on the left is sneaking up in back of you. Then there's the guy who's sitting on his horn, trying to get you to move over. And you wonder if the ambulance you hear is coming after you or somebody else.

Since you're not quite sure where to turn off, you keep looking at all the signs, and you miss the one you're looking for. Then, all of a sudden it begins to drizzle. Before long your windshield wipers are going like a hundred hands in a Swiss clock shop.

At that very moment when you feel you can't take any more, your mate asks you a question. Right then, one of the kids begins to holler about something and you find you have a disagreement going on in the back seat. If that weren't enough, you turn on the radio and learn that the stock market has plummeted another five points, that one of your favorite national heroes has just died, that war has broken out again in the Mid-East and that another typhoon has hit an island in the Pacific. Then the announcer says that the rain has been so heavy in the area just ahead of you, that all cars are having to take a detour. By that time your head is aching, your eyes are twitching, your neck is stiffening, your hands are cramping, your eyelids are blinking, and indeed, you could use a little bit of Sally Jones' advice on relaxing!

It wouldn't be so bad if this just happened once or twice a year. But it doesn't. Something like this seems to go on day after day in your car or at the office or at home. Indeed, what you and I need, is to develop an attitude of relaxation. And as Sally Jones so well explained, some of it may be in our heads!

So often when I'm driving along in my car I find myself squeezing the steering wheel much tighter than I should. So I say to myself, "Remember what Sally Jones said. Just relax and loosen your grip. Let your hand, wrist and arm take it easy." And if you're like me, while driving you suddenly wake up to the fact that your neck is rigid, and that your shoulder muscles are tight.

At this point, what can you do? The fact is, you can actually improve these situations by being aware that you *are* uptight, then suddenly relaxing.

The same thing applies to your work in the office. You may be typing, writing, answering the phone, running some machine, or doing a dozen other things. But all through the day you can ask yourself, "Am I really relaxing?" Then you can change your position a little, consciously let your muscles relax, and in a moment's time you can feel altogether differently.

As a homemaker you may be straining to do this or that, and before you realize it you are stiff and rigid, and uptight. Like everyone else you need to relax if you are to avoid undue pressure and tension. This attitude of mind can help you all day long, and in many ways. You can even get uptight thinking about the fact that you are going to have to do something that will *make* you feel uptight! You can be anticipating something and instead of anticipating it as an experience of relaxation, you can think of it as something which will cause you to be tired and filled with tension. So just thinking about what's going to happen can cause tension.

For example, I used to get myself into a little tension stew thinking about a trip which I was going to have to take. I have always enjoyed flying to various cities to speak at seminars and conventions. But these trips can be very tiring and on occasions I have returned home feeling like I'd been through the wringer.

Then, one day I thought to myself, "A lot of this is in my mind. This trip is not going to be a tension-producing trip; it's going to be a relaxing one. I'm going to think about it in a new way. I'm going to leave my home on Friday morning and go to the International Airport in Los Angeles. The ride there will be enjoyable. If I take my car, I'll talk with my wife and laugh, and have a good time. If, on the other hand, I take the airport bus, I won't have to drive, and I'll just relax, read, think, or do some other relaxing thing. Then on the plane, I'll relax again. In fact, I'll relax all the way to Boston, or to Atlanta, or to wherever. When arriving at the hotel room, I'll relax again, even if only for a few minutes. Then when Mr. Smith comes to the hotel to take me to the convention center, I'll relax while riding along in his car. When we arrive at the convention center and I go to the podium to speak, I'll be on my toes mentally, but I'm going to relax physically. While speaking I'll remember to relax my toes and shoulders. Then when I return to California on the plane I'll relax for several hours. Finally, I'll arrive back home relaxed, and ready to go to the office—feeling just fine!"

So I took the trip. I approached each part of it in an attitude of relaxation. I forgot a few times—but not many. And I actually relaxed most of the time! It was one of the most enjoyable trips I had ever taken. It was also the beginning of many more relaxing trips.

Here's the point: Much of what we do in life depends upon our attitudes. We can dread nearly everything, or we can see possibilities in those same things.

So it is with pressure. We can approach situations in an "uptight" manner, c. we can be alert to, and look for opportunities to relax. We can, to a great extent, train ourselves to relax in nearly all situations. And if we work at it long enough, it will become a habit. All of us can relax more by training ourselves to be conscious of relaxing. Indeed, a lot of it is in our approach; it's often in our head!

16. The Ultimate

In the foregoing chapters we have discussed many factors which could cause a person to feel tense and pressured. Some were medical in nature; others were psychological. These two extensive areas cover a lot of territory.

We've also talked about awareness, organization and management, and how they affect pressure in life. But there is another area which is even more significant and far reaching than these: *it is the spiritual*.

If human beings were merely physiological and psychological beings, there would be no spiritual causes of problems. But since people *are* spiritual beings, they do have spiritual problems; and of course, there are spiritual solutions. In fact, you cannot think about human beings in a scientific manner unless you take into consideration all three aspects of man; physiological, emotional and spiritual. If you leave any one of these out of your thinking, you are not facing all the facts; you *are unscientific in your approach*.

The Great Designer

Here is an evident fact: If God made human beings, then surely He is the One, and the only One, who knows perfectly how they function, and how they should function well. If a man had invented a complex machine, then that inventor would know precisely how the machine should function; how it shall be kept in order and running well.

There is no solid evidence in the world that man came into being except through the direct act of God. Untold millions of dollars have been spent on research and projects devoted to discounting the biblical explanation of the origin of man. For centuries, unbelievers have been digging around, in an attempt to come up with a bone or two that would lend some weight to their flimsy theories. But with all of this effort, nothing of any consequence has been unearthed relating to where man came from. As one of my professors at Columbia University once said, "I'm certainly not a religionist; but I must admit that in all my research and inquiry, I've never found any evidence that man came from anything except another man who was equal or superior to man today."

God's creation of man is described, "Let us make man in our image, after our likeness: and let them have dominion over the fish of the sea, and over the fowl of the air. . .So God created man in his own image, in the image of God created he him; male and female created he them" (Genesis 1:26, 27).

It stands to reason, then, that if we want to function in life with a minimum amount of pressure, God is our prime resource. He is the final authority on how a human being should live so that he is at his best.

As we study God's Word, the Bible, we find there are two basic areas we must explore to understand how a person can live with a minimum of pressure. The first concerns our *personal relationship with God*. Otherwise we cannot understand the Bible, which God has prepared for his people. Speaking of the "natural" or unsaved man, God says, "But the natural man receiveth not the things of the Spirit of God; for they are foolishness unto him, neither can he know them, because they are spiritually discerned (1 Corinthians 2:14).

The second is to study and obey the Word of God. In this way we can have the benefit of God directing our lives and bringing us stability and serenity.

One Bridge

Man in the twentieth century, just as men in all other periods, has one way available to him to establish a personal relationship with God, and have forgiveness of sins. The Bible clearly teaches that man is a spiritual being, made in the likeness of God. The opening chapters of the book of Genesis tell us that because of man's disobedience to God in the Garden of Eden, sin came upon the scene and began to plague all nature and all mankind. Sinful man then became separated from a righteous God. And man no longer enjoyed his intimate relationship with God. "Wherefore, as by one man sin entered into the world, and death by sin; and so death passed upon all men, for that all have sinned" (Romans 5:12).

But God has created man, among other things, for his fellowship. And it is only natural to believe that God would not be thwarted in his original plan to have his creatures relate to Him, worship Him and fellowship with Him. So God prepared a go-between: "For there is one God, and one mediator between God and man, the man Christ Jesus" (1 Timothy 2:5). It is important to know, too, that although this "way" is big enough for all mankind, it is the *only* way. Otherwise the death of Christ for the punishment of sin would have been a farce, and it would have been in vain. "Neither is there salvation in any other; for there is no other name under heaven given among men, whereby we must be saved" (Acts 4:12).

What does this have to do with pressures in everyday life?

A lot; a tremendous lot! When a man recognizes that he is a sinner, and he asks Christ to forgive him and enter into his heart, God immediately saves that man. "For God so loved the world that he gave his only begotten son, that whosoever believeth on him should not perish, but have everlasting life" (John 3:16).

When a person is saved, God's Holy Spirit immediately makes His abode in that person. And God gives him a new nature. He has new attitudes, new aspirations, new hopes and everything begins to be different. "Therefore if any man be in Christ, he is a new creature: old things are passed away; behold all things are become new" (2 Corinthians 5:17).

This new nature is only part of the benefits. As a person continues to follow Jesus Christ, to read God's Word, and to obey it, many more beneficial changes take place. And this tremendous process continues every day he lives. This really makes a difference, especially when it comes to pressure. You're thinking and living in tune with God!

If we were to fully explore all the ways in which the dynamic life in Christ can affect pressure in life, even several volumes could not contain it all. Nothing known to man can produce such beneficial results as a life that is directed by and energized by Christ. He is all, and in all. "For in him we live and move and have our being" (Acts 17:28).

Your Heavenly Father

One day I was conducting a seminar for business and professional men and their wives in the Philadelphia area. Throughout the day various participants mentioned how their lives and attitudes had been changed since the time they trusted in Christ as their personal Savior. Finally, during the afternoon break, a businessman came up to me on the platform and said, "Say, can I ask you a personal question?"

Then with all seriousness this man continued, "From what these people say, they know for sure that they're saved. Now my question is, how can a person be sure that he is saved, that he has a personal relationship with God?"

I explained that there were really only a few basic reasons why God gave us the Holy Scriptures. One was to show us how to have a personal relationship with Him, and another was to make it possible for us to *know* that we had it. And, of course, the Bible was also written so that after we have this life, and we know we have it, we can grow in Christ and be more effective, happier people.

"Well I don't know whether I'm saved or not," he said.

So I had the privilege (the greatest privilege a man can have) of showing this gentlemen just how he could be saved and how he could *know* he was saved.

First we looked at the fact that he, like all others, was a sinner. Then I pointed out Scripture showing that Jesus Christ God's Son, came into the world to save sinners. Next, I explained that as we *receive* Him, He comes into our hearts and gives us a new nature. Then we looked at several portions of Scripture. "That if you confess with your mouth Jesus as Lord, and believe in your heart that God raised Him from the dead, you shall be saved; for with the heart man believes, resulting in righteousness, and with the mouth he confesses, resulting in salvation" (Romans 10:9, 19). "For whoever will call upon the name of the Lord will be saved" (Romans 10:13).

This man was beginning to see that the authority for all spiritual matters is the Bible. And that when it clearly teaches a doctrine you can be sure of it and no one can refute it.

Like this man, as you trust Christ as Savior, you have a relationship going for you. You become God's son, and God becomes your father.

As a believer in Jesus Christ, you are in God's family. God is your *father* and you are his *son*. Mind boggling? Yes, but true! "Beloved, now we are children of God, and it has not appeared as yet what we shall be. We know that, if He should appear, we shall be like Him, because we shall see Him just as He is" (1 John 3:2). This relationship with your Creator and Savior lifts many burdens. You're not going it alone. It helps to relieve the pressure.

A Clean Slate

As a psychologist I am aware of many of the books written about guilt. Volumes line the shelves of our libraries. Students are required to read them.

Psychology students pore over them. Bibliographies are filled with them. Tests and examinations refer to them.

Why?

Because man is preoccupied with his guilt and sin. And as I have so often said, sin is a reality and it must be dealt with in a real way. We know, of course, that some people have been made to feel guilty by unthinking parents and others who influenced them in childhood. But this is only a small part of the story. Man *is* sinful. He *has* transgressed the laws of God. And one of his greatest sins is his rejection of God, and His Son, Jesus Christ.

Unlike those who are not saved, Christ has borne your sins on the cross of Calvary. He says He will remember your sins no more. You have a clean slate. "If we confess our sins, he is faithful and righteous to forgive us our sins and to cleanse us from all unrighteousness" (1 John 1:9). Nothing, absolutely nothing, is so debilitating as sin and guilt. It sucks the energy right out of you. It ruins today and it dulls tomorrow. It leaves your hopes and dreams in shambles.

But life doesn't have to be this way. You can have complete, irrevocable pardon! As God says, "Their sins and iniquities will I remember no more." You don't have to toil under a load of guilt and shame. This really takes off the pressure.

He Dwells Within

As one who knows Christ personally, you are indwelt by the Holy Spirit. This Holy Helper makes it easier to make adjustments to change, and to live a peaceful life with less pressure. The Bible teaches, "Or do you not know that your body is a temple of the Holy Spirit who is in you, whom you have from God, and that you are not your own? For you have been bought with a price: therefore glorify God in your body" (1 Corinthians 6:19, 20).

Indeed, God's Holy Spirit within you is available to correct you, to teach you, and to comfort you. You don't have to bear the tensions of your environment.

The average intelligent person is concerned about world conditions. And he should be. Reports from TV, radio newscasts, morning newspapers and many other sources are not all good; most of them are bad. But God has a great program going on, and you and I are in that program. As a believer in Christ you understand the times as taught in the Word of God. And the Holy Spirit which dwells within you, gives you understanding and peace. Before leaving this earth Christ said, "Peace I leave with you, my peace I give unto you not as the world giveth, give I unto you. Let not your heart be troubled, neither let it be afraid" (John 14:27).

Speaking of the peace which we can have when we live in Christ and keep our minds and hearts on God, the Bible says, "Thou wilt keep him in perfect peace, whose mind is stayed on thee, because he trusteth in thee" (Isaiah 26:3).

Your Caring Family

At the close of World War II, I received orders, as a naval officer, to go to Iceland for a few months. So I immediately contacted a Christian man whom I'd known previously, and who had lived in Iceland. I told him about the new move which I was making.

A few days after I arrived in Iceland, I was happily surprised to meet a business man in Reykjavik. He said that a Christian friend of his in the United States had written him saying that I was to be stationed there.

Before long, this Christian businessman introduced me to other Christians. Then they asked me to speak at one of their gatherings. Before many weeks had passed, I had a whole host of friends there in Iceland. I had visited them in their homes and they had visited me at the naval base. They were some of the warmest and most enthusiastic Christian people I had ever known. A few months earlier I hardly even knew where Iceland was, much less to have any friends there. Now, as a believer in Christ, I found that I had many brothers and sisters in that tiny nation of the North.

That's the way it is in the Christian life; you are never alone. All over the world, whether you are acquainted with them personally, or not, you have a wonderful family that prays for you and really cares about you.

Just as you are a blood-bought child of God, so there are millions of others who know Christ personally. Wherever you go throughout the world you will find those who have a kindred spirit and who love the same Savior. These fellow believers will reach out to you and reinforce you. They'll shepherd you, and share with you. They will bear many of your burdens and eliminate many stresses of life.

Uncommon Power

Pressure often builds up because you feel you're not equal to the job. God will not only lead you into those things which you should do; He will also give you the power to do them.

147
THE ULTIMATE

You are not a "nothing" helplessly floating around. You are a tremendous unit of effective power. Through Christ you can do what you ought to do, and you can refrain from doing what you should *not* be doing!

As a blood-bought Christian you can believe and experience the truth of the Bible: "I can do all things through Him who strengthens me" (Philippians 4:13). You don't have to stretch unduly, because He will help you reach your goals if they are in line with Him. You don't have to bend unduly because He gives you power to lift your loads. And the beautiful part of this fact is that it is available to you every day that you live!

You can walk with poise and confidence down life's road, because you are serving a sovereign God. You are not apprehensive about the outcome. "And Jesus came up and spoke to them, saying, "All authority has been given to Me in heaven and on earth" (Matthew 28:18).

God has a plan for your life, and you know that sinful men will meet their own destruction. You don't have to worry about straightening out the world. Your job is to be faithful. This attitude is effective in eliminating many of the struggles and tensions in life.

A Special Set of Keys

As a believer in Christ you are a pretty special person to God. Whereas the unsaved man cannot accept (or even understand) spiritual matters, God's Holy Spirit is your key to the Scriptures and to the life in Christ. "But a natural man does not accept the things of the Spirit of God; for they are foolishness to him, and he cannot understand them, because they are spiritually appraised" (1 Corinthians 2:14).

You have a special detection device, which is God's presence within you. As a result, you can discern many things which are not discernible by the unsaved person. Take, for example, current events and world conditions. You are not unduly uptight about things going on around the world because the Holy Spirit enables you to unlock the Scriptures. As you study God's Word, He will give you peaceful understanding. "And as for you, the anointing which you received from Him abides in you, and you have no need for anyone to teach you; but as His anointing teaches you about all things, and is true and not a lie, and just as it has taught you, you abide in Him" (1 John 2:27).

It is not absolutely necessary that you be surrounded by teachers, because the One who has *saved* you will also teach you God's truth. This cosmic type of understanding and spiritual perspective gives you unusual poise amid struggles and confusion that would otherwise bring on pressure.

Immediate Access

Much of the pressure in life can be eliminated as you turn immediately to God for help with both big and small concerns. And that is exactly what you should do. "Let us therefore draw near with confidence to the throne of grace, that we may receive mercy and may find grace to help in time of need" (Hebrews 4:16).

To put it plainly, you have a hot line to God Himself. This immediate prayer access can eliminate much sweat and tears. It will turn urgencies into opportunities.

As a finite being, it is only natural to worry about your everyday needs as well as the needs of your family and friends.

But God is in the provision business. All things were created by Him, and actually all things belong to Him. I believe it delights the heart of God to meet the needs of His children. "And my God shall supply all your needs according to His riches in glory in Christ Jesus" (Philippians 4:19). God can work in your heart in such a way that He will cause you to have *the right kind* of desires. Then He will graciously give you the godly desires of your heart. God's good gifts will come at the right time for you if you live in His presence, and develop the habit of waiting patiently and confidently on Him. This takes away unnecessary struggle and worry.

Motives and Priorities

As you trust in Christ and learn to live each day for Him, He will wonderfully change your motives and ambitions.

As one man said, "Three months after I was saved, I looked in the mirror and couldn't believe it was me!" This man had come to dislike his former life and had grown to love the things of Jesus Christ. A Jewish man once said to me, "Before I came to know Christ as my Messiah, I had two goals in life. I wanted to help my family, and I wanted to make all the money I possibly could. But now I look at things very differently. Naturally, I still want to be a blessing to my family. But the money, well, that's all changed. I have no compulsion to get more and more. Instead, I'm interested in telling others about Jesus. And I find great pleasure in helping support Christian ministries.

This man was delivered from a whole world of competition and stress. No longer was he intent on getting in another dollar. Instead, he was relaxing in the Lord, because God had changed his motives and ambitions. And this is true with everyone who goes for God in a surrendered, dedicated way.

In a sense, life keeps handing us a list of opportunities and responsibilities. *But we must decide on priorities*. Going into partnership with God helps here. As we devote each day to Him, He will guide us to the real priorities. In this way we can distinguish between the important and the unimportant, and we will not be filling each day with pressure.

Someone Who Cares and Guides

As you go about your daily work, many people will not understand you, much less *care* about you. Most people are busy with their own little worlds, not yours or mine. And most people are rather short on natural love for others. Not long ago I was talking with a Christian lady who told about a real disappointment she had recently experienced. In her neighborhood there lived a man who never extended himself to other people, and who was generally disliked. One day this man died suddenly. So the Christian neighbor bought a sympathy card and took it around the neighborhood to get people to sign it. Much to her surprise, she could get hardly anyone to sign the card. One woman seemed to sum it up when she blurted out, "We're *not* sorry he's dead; we're glad to get rid of him."

And so there is much hatred and selfishness in the hearts of many. Yet we know that it is important for individuals to be loved and understood and cared for.

God does just this, because you're the apple of His eye. "Casting all your anxiety upon him, because he cares for you" (1 Peter 5:7).

God knows all about you and He still likes you, and you're not going to stop Him! This eternal truth does away with a lot of pain and pressure.

As a follower of Jesus Christ you have the best and only reliable guide in the universe. He made it. "For such is God, our God forever and ever; He will guide us until death" (Psalm 48:14). If you seek His daily guidance He will keep you from making many wrong decisions, and He will guide you into paths of purity and progress. You don't have to go through life on a rough, winding detour. He will make your path straight; He will sprinkle it with joy and success, and He will furnish you peace, rather than pressure!

Your Destination

A Christian businessman was once asked to speak to a college class. After chatting with the students for a few minutes, he posed a question which got them to thinking about eternal values.

"What do you finally expect to do?" he asked.

Most of the students said they expected to graduate from college, get married and have a business or professional career.

"And after that?" the man enquired.

Then came such answers as "raise my family" or "make money" or "be successful."

"And what do you plan to do after that?" he asked.

Some of the students came up with the answer, "Eventually I'll die."

"And after that?" pressed the guest speaker.

Most of the class had nothing more to say. Then the speaker pointed out the great fact: "And as it is appointed unto men once to die, but after this the judgment" (Hebrews 9:27).

The final destination of man is a continual source of dread and fear to him. He goes to all extremes to force death out of his conscious thinking. So much of the entertainment and activities of life are actually designed, or at least engaged in, to prevent us from thinking about our eternal destiny. Yet, thoughts of dying hover over people, bringing worry and pressure.

As a born-again believer, you are headed in a new direction. Before your salvation you were walking toward a Christless eternity. But now you are walking toward your home in heaven which is being prepared for you. "Let not your heart be troubled; believe in God, believe also in me. In my Father's house are many dwelling places; if it were not so, I would have told you; for I go to prepare a place for you. And if I go and prepare a place for you, I will come again, and receive you unto myself; that where I am, there you may be also" (John 14:1-3).

You know, as a born-again believer, that when you leave this earth you will be in God's presence forever. "We are confident I say, and willing rather to be absent from the body, and to be present with the Lord" (2 Corinthians 5:8).

Indeed, your heart need not be troubled. You can walk with peace and decorum, because you realize that the earth is a "passing-through place," and that the burdens of life will soon be gone.

This takes off the pressure not only for now, but for eternity!